The Princeton Review

k12.princetonreview.com

Know It A

Grades 6–8 Reading

by Russell Kahn

Random House, Inc.
New York

www.randomhouse.com/princetonreview

...s written by The Princeton Review, one of the
... test preparation. The Princeton Review helps
...s every year prepare for standardized assessments
...inceton Review offers the best way to help students
...ized tests.

The Princeton Review is not affiliated with Princeton University or Educational
Testing Service.

Princeton Review Publishing, L.L.C.
160 Varick Street, 12th Floor
New York, NY 10013

E-mail: textbook@review.com

Published in the United States by Random House, Inc., New York.

ISBN 0-375-76379-1

Editor: Jennifer Humphries
Development Editor: Sherine Gilmour
Production Editor: Diahl Ballard
Director of Production: Iam Williams
Design Director: Tina McMaster
Art Director: Neil McMahon
Production Manager: Mike Rockwitz
Illustrations by Paulo De Freitas Jr.

Manufactured in the United States of America

9 8 7 6 5 4 3 2 1

First Edition

Dedication

To Mom, Dad, and Jordan. And of course my bride-to-be, Bethy.

Acknowledgments

There were many talented people involved in putting this book and this series together.

Thanks to Rachael Nevins, Scott Bridi, Sherine Gilmour, and Jodi Weiss for their help in developing the *Know It All!* concept and fine-tuning the elements of the series.

Thanks to Jennifer Humphries, my editor, for keeping my ideas in check and for being kind during the entire process.

Thanks to Reed Talada and Barbara Heinssen for giving me the opportunity to write this book and providing support.

Thanks to Diahl Ballard for her eagle-eyed copyedit and to Kristen Azzara for helping to coordinate the schedules.

Thanks to Neil McMahon and Peov for the art direction and creation of the fun and imaginative art in this book.

Thanks to Tina McMaster, Mike Rockwitz, and Greta Englert for crafting the creative layout and design.

And finally, thanks to the other *Know It All!* editors— Robert Elstein, Linda Fan, Michael Bagnulo, and Julia Munemo—as well as everyone else at The Princeton Review. Their dedication to student success is an inspiration.

Contents

Introduction for Parents and Teachers

About This Book

Know It All! focuses on the reading skills that students need to succeed in school and on standardized achievement tests while providing accurate information about a wide array of fascinating subjects.

Know It All! contains chapters that cover important reading skills, regular reviews called Brain Boosters, a practice test, and answers. Each **chapter** focuses on a skill or set of related skills, such as vocabulary in context or main idea, summary, and theme. The **practice test** was created to resemble the style, structure, difficulty level, and skills common in actual standardized achievement tests. The **answers** offer explanations to the questions on the practice test.

Each **chapter** contains the following:

- an introduction that presents and defines the chapter's skill(s)

- a step-by-step explanation of how to apply the chapter's skill(s), demonstrated with an example passage and question

- practice passages about interesting subjects and practice multiple choice and open-ended questions focusing on the chapter's skill(s)

- *Know It All!* tips to assist students in further developing their skills

There will also be cumulative "Brain Boosters" every three or four chapters to review new skills.

The **practice test** contains the following:

- passages similar in length and difficulty to passages on actual standardized achievement tests

- multiple-choice and open-ended questions similar in wording and difficulty to questions on actual standardized achievement tests

- a bubble sheet, similar to bubble sheets on actual standardized achievement tests, for students to fill in their answers to multiple-choice questions

Explanations following the practice test illustrate the best methods to solve each question.

About The Princeton Review

The Princeton Review is one of the nation's leaders in test preparation. We prepare more than two million students every year with our courses, books, online services, and software programs. We help students around the country on many statewide and national standardized tests in a variety of subjects and grade levels. Additionally, we help students on college entrance exams such as the SAT-I, SAT-II, and ACT. Our strategies and techniques are unique and, most importantly, successful. Our goal is to reinforce skills that students have been taught in the classroom and to show how to apply these skills to the format and structure of standardized tests.

About Standardized Achievement Tests

Across the nation, different standardized achievement tests are being used in different locations to assess students. States choose what tests they want to administer and, often, districts within the state also choose to administer additional tests. Some states administer state-specific tests, which are tests given only in that state and linked to that state's curriculum. Examples of state-specific tests are the Florida Comprehensive Assessment Test (FCAT) or the Massachusetts Comprehensive Assessment System (MCAS) exam. Other states administer national tests, which are tests used in several states in the nation. Examples of some national tests are the Stanford Achievement Test (SAT9), Iowa Test of Basic Skills (ITBS), and TerraNova/CTBS (Comprehensive Test of Basic Skills). Some states administer both state-specific tests and national tests.

Go to http://www.nclb.gov/next/where/statecontacts.html to find out more information about state-specific tests. You can also click on "Assessment Advisor" from the Web site http://k12.princetonreview.com.

Most tests administered to students contain multiple-choice and open-ended questions. Some tests are timed; others are not. Some tests are used to determine if a student can be promoted to the next grade; others are not.

To find out about what test(s) your student will take, when the test(s) will be given, if the test is timed, if it affects grade promotion, or other questions, contact your school or your local school district.

None of the tests can assess all of the unique qualities of your student. They are intended to show how well a student can apply skills they have learned in school in a testing situation.

Because they are connected to a state curriculum, state-specific tests show how well students can apply the curriculum that was taught in their school in a testing situation.

National tests are not connected to a specific state's curricula but have been created to include content that most likely would be taught in your student's grade and subject. Therefore, a national test may test content that has not been taught in your student's grade or school. National tests show how well a student has done on the test in comparison to other students in the nation have taken that same test.

Student Introduction

Student Introduction

About This Book

What kind of person is a *know it all*? Someone who craves information and wants to learn new things. Someone who wants to be amazed by what they learn. Someone who is excited by the strange and unusual.

Know It All! is an adventure for your mind. *Know It All!* is chock-full of wild, weird, zany, fascinating, unbelievable, and monumental articles—all of which contain true information! Plan to be stunned, amused, intrigued, and grossed out on this adventure.

In addition to feeding your brain all sorts of interesting information, *Know It All!* will give you test-taking tips and standardized test practice.

By the end of this book, you will have the biggest, strongest brain you've ever had! You'll be ready for a Brain Olympics or to become the president of the United Brains of the Universe. You'll be a *know it all!*

Know It All! contains **chapters, brain boosters,** and a **practice test.**

Each **chapter**
- defines a skill or group of skills, such as the chapter about vocabulary in context or the chapter about summary, main idea, and theme
- shows how to use these skills to answer an example question
- provides practice passages and questions like those you may see on standardized tests in school
- gives *Know It All!* tips to help you become the *know it all* you want to be

Each **brain booster**
- reviews the previous few skills
- includes a fun and interesting reading passage

The **practice test**
- provides passages similar in length and difficulty to passages on standardized tests
- gives questions similar in wording and difficulty to questions on standardized tests
- has a bubble sheet that is similar to the type on standardized achievement tests (to help you become an expert at bubble sheets)

You will also receive answers to the questions in the chapters and brain boosters. Also, you will get answers and explanations to the questions in the practice test.

About Standardized Achievement Tests

Standardized Achievement Tests. Who? What? Where? When? Why? How?

You know about them. You've probably taken them. But you might have a few questions about them. If you want to be a *know it all*, then it would be good for you to know about standardized achievement tests.

The words *standardized* and *achievement* describe the word *tests. Standardized* means to compare something with a standard. Standardized tests often use standards that have been decided by your school, district, or state. These standards list the skills you will learn in different subjects in different grades. *Achievement* means the quality of the work produced by a student, a heroic act, or an impressive result gained through effort. So *standardized achievement tests* are tests that assess the quality of your work with certain skills. According to these definitions, you can consider yourself an impressive hero for all of your efforts.

To find out the nitty-gritty about any standardized achievement tests you may take, ask your teachers and/or parents. Here are some questions you might want to ask.

Who?	You!
What?	What kinds of questions will be on the test? What kinds of skills will be tested?
Where?	Where will the test happen?
When?	When will the test happen? How much time will I have to complete the test?
Why?	Why do I have to take the test? What is the purpose of the test?
How?	How should I be prepared? Do I need to bring anything to the test? If I don't know the answer to a question, should I guess?

None of the tests can assess your unique qualities as a *know it all.* They are intended to show how well you can use the skills that you learned in school in a testing situation.

About the Icons in This Book

This book contains many different small pictures, called icons. The icons tell you about the topics in the articles in the book.

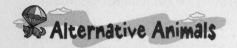 **Alternative Animals**

Read these passages to learn about animals that you never knew existed and feats that you never knew animals could accomplish. You'll learn about the biggest, smallest, oldest, fastest, and most interesting animals on the planet. You can find these passages in chapters 1, 6, 8, 11, and 14.

 **Extreme Sports**

Read these passages to learn about outrageous contests, wacky personalities, and incredible feats in the world of sports. You may not have even heard of some of these sports! You can find these passages in chapters 3, 7, 8, and 15.

 **Hip History**

Your mission is to storm some of the coolest castles in history with some extraordinary historical figures—some of whom aren't much older than you. These passages will help you complete that mission while learning the most interesting stories in history. You can find these passages in chapters 2, 9, and 10.

 **Grosser Than Gross**

How gross can you get? Read these passages if you want to learn about really gross things. Be warned: Some of the passages may be so gross that they're downright scary. You can find these passages in chapters 4 and 7.

 **For Your Amusement**

You want to play games? Read these passages to learn about cool games, toys, amusement parks, and festivals. You can find these passages in chapters 4, 6, and 12.

 **Mad Science**

If you read these passages, you'll see science like you've never seen it before. You'll learn about all sorts of interesting science-related stuff. You can find these passages in chapters 3, 5, 11, and 14.

 ## Outer Space Oddities

Do you ever wonder what goes on in the universe away from planet Earth? Satisfy your curiosity by reading these passages about astronomical outer-space oddities. You can find these passages in chapters 8 and 16 and in Brain Boosters 1 and 3.

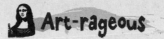 ## Art-rageous

Are you feeling a bit creative? Read these passages to get an unusual look into art that's all around you: books, drawings, paintings, and much more. You can find these passages in chapters 3, 9, 13, and 16.

 ## Explorers and Adventurers

Did you ever want to take a journey to learn more about a place? Well, you'll get the opportunity to do that if you read these passages about explorers and adventurers. You can find these passages in chapters 2, 5, 12, and 16.

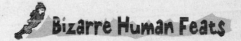 ## Bizarre Human Feats

People do some very strange stuff. You can read about some of these incredible-but-true human feats in these passages. You can find these passages in chapters 4 and 6 and in Brain Boosters 2 and 4.

The Entertainment Center

Do you enjoy listening to music or watching television and movies? Well, here's your chance to read about them! You can find these passages in chapters 2, 11, 14, and 15.

 ## WILD CARDS

You'll never know what you're going to get with these passages. It's a mixed bag. Anything goes! You can find these passages in chapters 1, 5, and 9 and in Brain Booster 5.

Things to Remember When Preparing for Tests

There are many things you can do to prepare for standardized achievement tests. Here are a few examples.

- **Work hard in school all year.** Working hard in school all year is a great way to prepare for tests.

- **Read.** Read everything you can. Reading a lot is a great way to prepare for tests.

- **Work on this book!** This book provides you with loads of practice for tests. You've probably heard the phrase, "Practice makes perfect." Practice can be a great way to prepare for tests.

- **Ask your teachers and/or parents questions about your schoolwork whenever necessary.** Your teachers and your parents can help you with your schoolwork. Asking for help when you need it is a great way to prepare for tests and to become a *know it all*.

- **Ask your teachers and/or parents for information about the tests.** If you have questions about the tests, ask! Being informed is a great way to prepare for tests.

- **Have good dinners and good breakfasts before the tests.** Eating well will fuel your body with energy, and your brain thrives on energy. You want to take a test with all the engines ready in your brain.

- **Get enough sleep before the tests.** Being awake and alert while taking tests is very important. Your body and your mind work best when you've had enough sleep. So get some Zs on the nights before tests!

- **Check your work.** When taking a test, you may end up with extra time. Use extra time to check your work, you might spot some mistakes—and improve your score.

- **Stay focused.** You may find that your mind has wandered away from the test once in a while. Don't worry—it happens. Just say to your brain, "Brain, it's great that you are so curious, imaginative, and energetic. But I need to focus on the test now." Your brain will thank you later.

Chapters

CHAPTER 1
Multiple-Choice and Open-Response Questions

Are killer bees coming to a town near you?

Why would anybody pay to sleep on a bed made of ice?

Did you know that there are really only two types of questions that you'll ever see on any reading test you'll ever take? It's true. Almost every question will be either **multiple choice** or **open response.** Learning different strategies for answering these questions can make your life as a test taker a million times easier.

Some tests contain only multiple-choice questions. Other tests contain only open-response questions. Still others contain a combination of both types of questions. You will be getting a lot of practice with both type of questions throughout this book.

When you see a multiple-choice question, you should jump for joy and scream at the top of your lungs. Why? Every multiple-choice question offers several answer choices from which you can choose the correct answer. The correct answer is always among the answer choices given. That means the correct answer is printed on the page, right in front of you. Your job is to figure out which answer choice is correct and which answer choices are incorrect. (Okay, maybe you don't really have to jump for joy and scream at the top of your lungs, but multiple-choice questions aren't so bad.)

On the other hand, when you see an open-response question, you don't need to weep. Open-response questions do not provide answers for you to choose from, but they do give you opportunities to express your own thoughts and ideas. You can get points for your opinions. Even if your final answer isn't totally correct, you can sometimes get partial credit for your answer. You will usually answer open-response questions on lines provided in a test or in a separate answer book. Sometimes you will answer open-response questions in a table or graph. Always answer these questions in complete sentences unless the directions tell you otherwise.

Starting on the next page, you will see a passage on killer bees followed by a sample multiple-choice question. The question will be followed with a way to find the right answer from the answer choices listed. An open-response question will follow later in this chapter.

Alternative Animals

Killer Bees: The Bees with a Bad Attitude

A killer bee looks like a common honeybee that you may have seen buzzing around a park or in a backyard near you. But unlike a common honeybee, which does not attack you unless you make it mad, a killer bee can attack for very little reason. Also, some killer bees attack in very large groups. People have been covered with killer bees and stung hundreds of times. Some people have even died from receiving multiple killer bee stings.

When killer bees sting and inject their venom into their victims, they also leave behind a special chemical. Other killer bees smell this chemical, and it makes them want to attack as well! This makes killer bees exceptionally dangerous.

Did you know that the deadly killer bee is a result of a twentieth-century science experiment gone wrong? It's true. In 1957, a Brazilian geneticist was performing experiments on certain species of African queen bees. He was trying to find a way to make a bee create more honey. Instead, the bees escaped into the wild. Uh-oh! The escaped bees mated with the common honeybee to create a new type of bee that was extremely aggressive.

Although killer bees originated in Brazil, they have spread north through Central America and Mexico. Recently, killer bees have been found in Texas, Arizona, New Mexico, Nevada, and California. Some scientists think they will continue to spread north throughout the United States. Others don't think they will. What will happen with killer bees in the future? Where else will they go? Only time will tell.

Here is a sample multiple-choice question about the passage *Killer Bees: The Bees with a Bad Attitude.*

▶ Where did killer bees originate?

A Arizona   C Mexico
B Australia   D Brazil

To answer multiple-choice questions, it helps to use the following steps.

Steps for Answering Multiple-Choice Questions

Step 1

Read the passage carefully.

Multiple-choice questions ask about passages that you have read. While reading each passage, underline important details or take notes in the margins. Take notes on a separate piece of paper if you are not allowed to write directly on the test.

Step 2

Read the question carefully.

Try to determine exactly what the question is asking. Words such as **not** or **except** usually ask you to find the answer choice that is not supported by the information from the passage. Words such as *effect* and *because* tell you that the question is asking about a cause-and-effect relationship.

Step 3

Think of the answer in your own words.

Before you choose from the answer choices provided, try to phrase the answer in your own words. Use only information that is provided in the passage. Go back and check the passage if necessary.

Step 4

Read all the answer choices.

Look for the answer choice that is most similar to the answer you came up with and that best answers the question. Even if you think you have found the correct answer choice, read all the choices to make sure there isn't a better one.

Step 5

For questions you are unable to answer, use Process of Elimination (POE).

If you use POE, you increase your odds of finding the correct answer to a difficult multiple-choice question. Even if you can't find the correct answer choice, you may be able to find the *incorrect answer choices.* For example, you may figure out that an answer choice is incorrect because it is not supported by the information from the passage. Draw a line through answer choices you *know* are incorrect. Then take your best guess from the remaining answer choices.

Know It All Approach

To answer this multiple-choice question, reread the passage and the question. If you haven't already, underline important details in the passage. Then decide what the question is asking. This one is asking the origin of killer bees.

Think of the answer in your own words. Refer to passage. You won't be expected to memorize a whole passage, so it's okay to go back for more information. The first sentence of the last paragraph gives a clue about the answer. It starts by saying "Although killer bees originated in Brazil . . .." This basically means that the answer to the question is probably "Brazil."

If you know the answer, circle the letter on your test and fill in the bubble on your answer sheet (if the test includes a separate bubble sheet). Even if you think you know the right answer, check all the choices anyway.

If you're having a hard time finding the correct answer, use Process of Elimination (POE). That means going through the answer choices one-by-one and crossing off any answer choices that you *know* are wrong. Consider the answer choices that are left. Pick the answer choice that is best supported by the information in the passage.

This question asked where killer bees originated. Arizona may look like a possible answer because the passage mentions Arizona. But be careful and check the passage: The passage doesn't say that's where they *originated*. They were just *found* in Arizona. Cross off (A) and move to the next answer choice. What about (B)? Did the passage say *anything* about Australia? Australia wasn't mentioned in the passage, so it can't be correct. Cross it off! What about (C)? The passage mentions that bees *traveled* across Mexico. They didn't originate from Mexico! Therefore, (C) is not correct. Draw a line through it! You're left with (D), Brazil. Check the passage. The last paragraph says "killer bees originated in Brazil" so, yes, (D) is correct.

Now here's an example of an open-response question about the killer bee passage.

► Describe how the Brazilian scientist probably felt after his bees escaped from his laboratory and became killer bees.

_____

_____

Steps for Answering Open-Response Questions

Step 1

Read the passage carefully.

While reading the passage, underline important details or take notes in the margins. If you aren't supposed to write on the test, take notes on a separate piece of paper.

Step 2

Read the question carefully.

Figure out exactly what the question is asking, such as *explain, describe, compare, contrast, both, because, different, similar,* and others.

Step 3

Plan your answer.

As you think about your answer, return to the passage and check your notes or underlined words. Use only information provided in the reading passage in your answer.

Step 4

Write your answer neatly and clearly.

Use complete sentences!

Step 5

Revise your answer.

Make sure that you answered the question completely, that you used details from the passage in your answer, and that you don't have any punctuation, spelling, or other technical errors.

Know It All Approach

This question asks you to describe how the scientist probably felt when his bees escaped from his lab, creating *killer bees.* Think about what you want to write and include details from the passage in your response.

The passage says that killer bees are very dangerous and that some people have died as a result of them. How would *you* feel if you unleashed this scary new animal on the world? Hopefully, you'd feel pretty bad about it.

Plan your answer. Think about *how* the scientist felt and *why* you think he felt that way. Write in complete sentences and revise. Below is a response that would most likely receive full credit.

The Brazilian scientist probably felt worried when his bees escaped from his lab

because the bees posed a serious danger to humans.

The Coolest Hotel: The Ice Hotel

Usually when you stay in a hotel, you expect to be comfortable, relaxed, cozy, and warm. But there is a hotel in Canada, near Quebec City, in which the temperature never gets above freezing. That's right; the average temperature in the Ice Hotel is a chilly 25 degrees Fahrenheit! That's a good thing, though. Why? If the hotel were much warmer, it would melt. The whole building is made entirely from snow and ice!

Snow and ice are used to create everything in the hotel, from the four-feet-thick walls to the chandeliers and drinking glasses. Even the beds are made out of ice! Could you imagine sleeping on a bed made of ice? Well, thousands of people don't have to imagine it—they've done it! Every year, the Ice Hotel attracts about 50,000 people, and more than 2,000 of them stay overnight on the beds of ice. Fortunately, the beds are covered with wooden planks, deer fur, and thick sleeping bags so that the guests don't turn into icicles over night!

The Ice Hotel has plenty of fun things to do; it includes a movie theater, a nightclub, and even a chapel—just in case people want to get married in the bitter cold. And if you were wondering about bathrooms, there is a separate (and heated) facility with running water.

Each year, workers use more than 11,000 tons of snow and 350 tons of ice to create the Ice Hotel. The hotel covers an area of about 30,000 square feet. It takes five weeks to build the hotel each year, and it is usually ready by early January. It closes in March when the weather warms up and the ice begins to thaw. When it closes, the hotel is dumped into a nearby lake. Every year they start over with a brand-new design and build a brand-new, completely different hotel.

Don't you wish *your* room were made out of big blocks of snow and ice?

Directions: Answer questions 1–4 based on the Ice Hotel reading passage.

1. What is one part of the Ice Hotel that is heated?

    A   the movie theater   C   the wedding chapel
    B   the bathrooms   D   the bedrooms

2. Write three items that that are made out of ice or snow that you could find in the Ice Hotel. Write your answer using complete sentences.

    _____

    _____

3. When is the Ice Hotel usually open?

    A   all year long
    B   from March through November
    C   from January through March
    D   only in the summer

4. Name two ways that the Ice Hotel tries to keep their guests warm when sleeping on a bed made of ice.

    _____

    _____

Subject Review

By now you should be familiar with both multiple-choice and open-response questions. You will be tackling each type of question in the chapters ahead. Now that you have finished Chapter 1, you can answer the following questions.

Are killer bees coming to a town near you?

Well, no one really knows the answer for sure, but killer bees are probably not coming to a town near you. Even though they are spreading northward from Brazil and are found in some southern and western states, killer bees aren't necessarily going to take over!

Why would somebody pay to sleep on a bed made of ice?

We don't know; people like to do strange things sometimes. But the Ice Hotel is a very unique place, and it has become a popular tourist attraction. Maybe these people just want to tell their friends, "Hey, I slept on a giant ice cube once."

CHAPTER 2
Details

How did a Viking's big, fat lie create Greenland's name?

How were flying cats used to attack an Egyptian city?

How did getting mugged help Mel Gibson's movie career?

Details are pieces of information in a reading selection. They tell you information or give a description using a single word or phrase. A detail can tell you that a person is short or tall, skinny or fat, a science brain like Einstein or a lover of literature like Shakespeare. Details can often tell you the order in which things happened (although we still don't know which came first: the chicken or the egg).

Supporting details are details that support the ideas in a passage. For example, an author writing a passage that says school should always be held at amusement parks would include details that support this idea. The author might note that "food and beverages are available at amusement parks, so students would not need to eat at the school cafeteria." Or the author might write that "amusement parks offer lots of activities that encourage students to exercise, so schools would not need to provide gym classes."

Read the two descriptions of a baseball pitcher below.

> *Zola lost the game.*

> *Defeated, Zola sighed heavily and lowered her head with resignation before walking slowly off the pitcher's mound.*

Both sentences tell you the same basic information: Zola lost the game. However, the first sentence does not have any details. It is also pretty boring to read. The second sentence gives you more information. It brings the situation to life and is more descriptive. Notice that the second sentence doesn't tell you exactly what the problem is, but all of the details tell you what the problem might be.

Read the passage about Erik the Red on the next page. Remember to pay attention to the details and take notes as you read. The passage will be followed with an open-response question and a Know It All Approach that shows how to answer it.

Explorers and Adventurers

Erik the Red: A Great Liar

Erik Thorvaldsson, a Viking nicknamed "Erik the Red" because of his red hair, murdered two men in Iceland in the year A.D. 980. He was found guilty of a crime and banished from his island home for three years. As a result, he left and sailed west, away from Iceland. He landed on the world's largest island, which is now known as Greenland.

Even though the island was covered in ice and snow, Erik the Red named it Greenland. He knew that nobody would want to come to a place with such harsh living conditions. So when Erik returned to Iceland, he told everyone that the land in Greenland was green and habitable. Based on his appealing descriptions, people wanted to go!

Erik the Red's lies were successful in getting many people to move to Greenland. One of Erik's sons, Leif Eriksson, later went on to become one of the world's most famous explorers.

▶ Why did Erik the Red travel to the land now known as Greenland?

_____

Know It All Approach

Check back on page 16 to review the steps for answering open-response questions. Read the passage and question carefully, and figure out exactly what you're supposed to do to answer the question. You need to identify why Erik the Red traveled to Greenland. Return to the passage for details.

Using information and details from the passage, plan your answer. The passage says that Erik the Red was banished from Iceland. As a result, he sailed west, where he discovered the island he later named Greenland.

Plan a clear response that provides details from the passage. Don't forget to write your response clearly in complete sentences. When you're done, be sure to revise your answer.

Below is a sample response that would receive full credit to this open-response question.

Erik the Red traveled to the land now known as Greenland because he was banished

from his home in Iceland.

The Odd, Early Days of Domestic Cats

Even if you're not the biggest cat fan in the world, chances are you know at least one person that's absolutely bonkers for their cat. Maybe they won't leave their cat alone overnight. Perhaps they won't stop talking about how cute Whiskers is. One thing is for sure: Cat owners love their cats. But no one loves their cat as much as the ancient Egyptians!

The history of the domesticated cat dates back to ancient Egypt, at least 3,500 years ago. Many people believe that wild cats were first domesticated as a way to protect the farms from rodents. Cats were sacred animals to the Egyptians.

Sometimes a person who killed a cat in ancient Egypt was sentenced to death as a punishment.

You've probably heard of mummies. Well, in ancient Egypt wealthy families not only mummified their human family members, but they also mummified cats to keep them company in the afterlife. Sometimes even mice were mummified so the kitties could eat in the afterlife!

Legend has it that cats even played a role in a defeat of the Egyptian army in 525 B.C. The Egyptian city of Memphis was under attack by King Cambyses of Persia and his army. Unfortunately for King Cambyses, he couldn't get past the giant wall that protected Memphis. Knowing that the Egyptians thought cats were sacred, so one version of the story goes, King Cambyses had his army gather hundreds of cats and throw them over the wall that protected Memphis. The Egyptians couldn't stand the sight of the cats being hurt, so they surrendered to save the cats' lives.

Directions: Answer questions 1–5 about the passage about the odd, early history of domesticated cats.

1. What was sometimes the penalty in ancient Egypt for killing a cat?

   A The offender had his or her hands cut off.
   B The offender was mummified.
   C The offender was sentenced to death.
   D The offender had to eat a mouse.

2. Domesticated cats have probably existed

   A since at least 1,500 B.C.
   B for about 1,000 years.
   C since at least 3,500 B.C.
   D for about 10,000 years.

3. Why were mummified mice included with mummified cats in their tombs?

   A to scare away possible intruders
   B to provide food for the cats in the afterlife
   C to protect the Egyptian farms
   D to give the mummies entertainment in heaven

4. What do many people believe was the reason that cats were domesticated?

   _____

   _____

5. What explanation does the passage give for the Persian army defeating the Egyptian city of Memphis?

   _____

   _____

The Entertainment Center

Mel Gibson's Lucky Break:
A Punch in the Face!

You might know actor Mel Gibson from such movies as *Signs, The Patriot, Braveheart,* or the *Lethal Weapon* series. He's one of the biggest stars in Hollywood today. He's also one of the highest paid stars, too, making as much as $25 million per film. However, it may be that a fistfight helped make him famous. How? Read on.

Mel Gibson was born in New York in 1956, but he and his family (ten brothers and sisters) moved to Australia when he was twelve. He went to college to study dramatic art in New South Wales, Australia, to learn acting. Later he worked as an actor in a variety of plays.

Gibson's big break came the day before his first screen test, which is a type of audition. He was involved in a fight during which he was beaten up and mugged. He had to go to the hospital. His face showed the scars of the brawl, with bruises and cuts all over it.

The next day, he auditioned for the Australian action film *Mad Max.* Even though Gibson didn't know it, the directors of the movie were seeking a strange-looking person who looked rugged and wounded. He was hired to play the leading role, but he probably would not have gotten the role if he looked clean and tidy! *Mad Max* came out in 1979 and became Australia's highest-grossing movie of all time. (That record was broken two years later by the sequel, *Mad Max: The Road Warrior,* also starring Mel Gibson.)

Eventually, Gibson started working on American films such as *The River* in 1984. His international appeal continued to grow with American movies like *Lethal Weapon,* and he now appears in all sorts of Hollywood blockbusters. He even added his voice to a handful of animated movies, such as Disney's *Pocahontas* and *Chicken Run.* One time, he recorded his voice for an episode of *The Simpsons*!

Gibson also directed several of the movies he starred in, starting with *The Man Without a Face* in 1993. In 1995, he even won a "Best Director" Academy Award for his work on *Braveheart,* a movie he acted in, directed, and produced. Whether or not you're a fan, Mel Gibson is one of the most multitalented entertainers in Hollywood.

Directions: Answer questions 6–10 about the Hollywood actor Mel Gibson.

6. Where was Mel Gibson born?

   A   Australia
   B   New South Wales
   C   New York
   D   Hollywood

7. What job has Mel Gibson **not** done in the movie business?

   A   voices in animated movies
   B   costume design
   C   directing
   D   producing

8. What was the first movie that Mel Gibson directed?

   A   *Mad Max: The Road Warrior*
   B   *The River*
   C   *The Man Without a Face*
   D   *Braveheart*

9. Which detail from the passage best supports the idea that Mel Gibson has many talents?

   A   *Mad Max* was Australia's highest-grossing movie of all time.
   B   Mel Gibson was born in New York in 1956, but he and his family moved to Australia when he was twelve.
   C   After the fight, Gibson's face showed the scars of the brawl, with bruises and cuts all over it.
   D   Gibson won a "Best Director" Academy Award for his work on *Braveheart,* a movie he acted in, directed, and produced.

10. Explain how a fight helped Mel Gibson win the leading role in *Mad Max.*

   _____

   _____

Subject Review

In this chapter, you learned that there are a few different kinds of details. Some help to paint a picture. Others help to support an idea. There is one feature that all types of details have in common: They are tested on exams!

You have to use details to find the correct answer choice for a multiple-choice question. You also have to use details to support your response to an open-response question. Using details is essential to getting a good score on any test you take.

Now you can answer the questions that began the chapter.

How did a Viking's big, fat lie create Greenland's name?
Erik the Red was banished from Iceland and sailed to the island now known as Greenland. As a way to get people to move to the giant island, he named it "Greenland" and lied about its hospitable environment. The country was not green at all, but instead it was almost entirely white with snow and ice!

How were flying cats used to attack an Egyptian city?
The Persian King Cambyses and his army couldn't get past the giant wall that protected Memphis. Knowing that the Egyptians thought cats were sacred, King Cambyses had his army throw hundreds of cats over the wall that protected Memphis. Because the Egyptians held cats sacred, they surrendered to save the cats' lives.

How did getting mugged help Mel Gibson's movie career?
The directors of *Mad Max* were looking for a person who looked rugged and wounded. Because he was beaten up the previous day, his cuts and bruises helped him to get hired to play the leading role!

CHAPTER 3
Vocabulary in Context

How many paintings did Vincent van Gogh paint in a day?

Is it healthy to have slimy, sticky, bloodsucking leeches attached to your body?

Can a man with one hand get a hit in major league baseball?

The more vocabulary words you know, the more you will understand what you read, the smarter you will sound when you talk, and the better you will do on standardized tests. It is also true that no one can ever know the meaning of every word. The trick is to use context to help you figure out what a word means. The **context** of a word is the information that surrounds it in the passage.

Read the following paragraph. It contains one word you have probably never heard before.

The first time I met Mongoose, I was in awe. He towered over me like a lighthouse. In fact, he was so tizzillwizzil that I barely stood up to his waist. I even had to reach up over my head to shake his enormous hand.

You have probably never heard the word *tizzillwizzil* before. That's because it's made up. Although the word doesn't exist, you can still figure out its meaning. Find the word *tizzillwizzil* in the paragraph, and then look at the words surrounding it. Mongoose was so *tizzillwizzil* that the writer barely stood up to his waist. The author had to reach up to shake his hand. What does that mean about Mongoose? If you only stood up to someone's waist, it means that he or she must be pretty tall. So, *tizzillwizzil* means tall. Mongoose must be tall.

Vocabulary-in-context questions ask you to determine the meaning of words in a passage by using the words, phrases, and information that surround them. You can use context to figure out what *tizzillwizzil* means and you can use context to find the meaning of real unfamiliar words. (By the way, don't use *tizzillwizzil* in front of your teacher. You might get some confused looks.)

Many vocabulary-in-context questions are multiple choice, meaning the correct definition is listed in one of a few answer choices. This is helpful because you can use those answer choices to your advantage. How? Just substitute the definitions from the answer choices into the unknown vocabulary word. Only one will work.

Read the example about Vincent van Gogh on the next page for more practice answering these questions.

 **Art-rageous**

Vincent van Gogh, Go, Go

You may know of Vincent van Gogh as the mentally disturbed painter who cut off his ear or as the brilliant impressionist artist who painted such masterpieces as *The Starry Night*. Whatever you may think about him, van Gogh's paintings are among the most prized in the world.

Van Gogh produced hundreds of paintings and drawings. However, his career only lasted about ten years. He was a speedy painter, and he produced a lot of artwork, considering the shortness of his career. In fact, he was so *prolific* that he painted a canvas every day for the last seventy days of his life. He died when he was thirty-seven.

▶ What does the word *prolific* mean in the second paragraph?

A   disturbed   C   old
B   talented   D   productive

Know It All Approach

Maybe you already know what the word *prolific* means. If not, don't worry. You can use context to figure out its meaning—and find the correct answer choice.

First find *prolific*, and then read the phrases that surround it. The word appears after you learn that he "was a speedy painter" and created a lot of artwork in only a few years. He was so *prolific* that he painted a canvas each day for seventy days.

Use the answer choices for help. Replace the word *prolific* with each of the answer choices to see which one makes sense in the passage.

Does (A) make sense? "Van Gogh was so *disturbed* that he painted a canvas every day for the last seventy days of his life." Well, van Gogh was disturbed enough to cut off his ear, but that doesn't explain why he painted so much. Cross off (A). Does (B) make sense? "Van Gogh was so *talented* that he painted a canvas every day." Sure, he was probably talented to paint so much. Hold on to this answer choice and try (C) and (D) to see if they're better.

Answer choice (C) says "Van Gogh was so *old* that he painted a canvas every day for the last seventy days of his life." That doesn't make sense. Plus, van Gogh wasn't old when he died! Cross off (C). Answer choice (D) says that "Van Gogh was so *productive* that he painted a canvas every day." That means he produced a lot of work. Yes, that's it exactly! (D) is a better answer choice than (B) because it fits the context more accurately.

Mad Science

I Want To Suck Your Blood—
For Your Own Good!

1   Modern medicine has sure come a long way. In case you want proof, consider the leech—one of the most popular tools of nineteenth-century medicine. Physicians used these creepy, wormlike, bloodsucking parasites for a practice called *bloodletting*. That meant that dozens of slimy leeches were placed on a patient's skin and allowed to suck their blood. This was believed to help rid the patient of bad blood, which could *alleviate* any number of illnesses, from headaches to mental illness.

2   You might think that leeches, with their hundreds of sharp little teeth and powerful jaws, are very dangerous animals. But the truth is that most leeches are *innocuous*. If you ever find one on your body, you can just let it stay there. It will drop off when it's finished eating, and you generally won't feel any pain. The slimy animals are also nice enough to try to *mend* your wound after they bite you and suck your blood.

3   If you watch a leech suck some blood, you will likely see it grow fat in only a few minutes. That's because a leech can *ingest* several times its own weight in blood at one meal. If you could do that, it would be like eating 200 pounds of pizza, hot dogs, and fries in one sitting.

4   Even though leeches are no longer used for bloodletting, they still serve a medicinal purpose. Because leeches suck blood from their victims, they can help stimulate blood flow. This blood flow is useful for surgeons who want to reconnect body parts.

5   In 1985, a five-year-old boy had his ear bitten off by a dog. The doctors reattached it, but the smaller veins in the ear were blocked. In an experimental effort, the doctors set twenty-four leeches on the boy's ear. The leeches helped to restore blood flow to the ear, which helped to heal it. It worked!

6   While leeches helped this particular boy *retain* his ear, they are rarely used in modern-day medicine. Still, it is nice to know that even the grossest-looking creatures can help humankind.

Directions: Answer questions 1–6 based on the passage about leeches.

1. In paragraph 1, what does the word *alleviate* mean?

   A hurt   C grow

   B painful   D improve

2. In paragraph 2, what does the word *innocuous* mean?

   A dangerous   C harmless

   B disgusting   D slimy

3. In paragraph 2, what word could be used instead of *mend*?

   A fix   C eat

   B hurt   D meet

4. In paragraph 3, what does the word *ingest* mean?

   A bite   C involve

   B eat   D help

5. Write one word that could replace the word *retain* in paragraph 6

   _____

6. On the lines below, explain what the word *bloodletting* means.

   _____

   _____

Jim Abbott: A Major-League Pitcher with a Difference

1   Even though he was born without a right hand, Jim Abbott was determined not to let his disability get in his way. As a young boy, he spent hours bouncing a ball off a wall to practice throwing and fielding. His *dogged* efforts paid off. By the time he was in high school, he was the starting quarterback on the football team. He was so *adept* that he took his team to the state championship.

2   After high school, Abbott went to the University of Michigan to play baseball. He pitched for the college's baseball team, winning twenty-six times and losing only eight times. Because he was left handed and pitched with his left hand, he was called a *southpaw*. He also pitched for the United States Olympic team in the 1988 Olympics. In fact, he was the winning pitcher in the game that brought the United States its first gold medal in baseball!

3   The California Angels drafted Abbott in the first round, meaning he was a very coveted player. The Angels never even put him in the minor leagues. He went straight to the major leagues, where he had a very good first season, winning a dozen games. A few years later, in 1991, he won eighteen games for the Angels, ending the season with a 2.89 ERA.

4   The *pinnacle* of Abbott's career, however, came when he played for the New York Yankees in 1993. Playing in Yankee Stadium, he threw a no-hitter against the Cleveland Indians. No-hitters are *scarce* in professional baseball; fewer than 300 players in the major leagues have ever had one before.

5   Abbott was also a very *competent* fielder. He could catch almost anything hit back to him. He wore a right-hander's glove on the stump of his right arm. After he threw a pitch, he would quickly switch the glove to his left hand to field his position. In 1999, the final season of his career, Abbott got his first major league hit for the Milwaukee Brewers.

Directions: Answer questions 7–12 based on the passage about Jim Abbott.

7. In paragraph 1, what does the word *dogged* mean?

   A lazy

   B defected

   C young

   D determined

8. In paragraph 1, what does the word *adept* mean?

   A skilled

   B average

   C inspirational

   D pitcher

9. In paragraph 4, what does the word *pinnacle* mean?

   A pitch

   B highlight

   C bottom

   D beginning

10. In paragraph 4, what word could be used instead of *scarce?*

    A great

    B rare

    C common

    D wonderful

11. Write one word that could replace the word *competent* in paragraph 6.

    _____

12. Explain what a *southpaw* is on the lines below.

    _____

    _____

Subject Review

Try to learn new words whenever possible, and always use context to help you with the words you don't know. A better vocabulary will help you on tests, such as the SAT, as well as on papers, and for the rest of your life.

By now you've seen how using context can help you understand tough vocabulary. By using the surrounding words and phrases, you can figure out the meaning of almost any word—even *tizzillwizzil,* which isn't a real word!

And now you can figure out the answers to the questions on page 27.

How many paintings did Vincent van Gogh paint in a day?

For an artist who died when he was only thirty-seven, he produced quite a lot of art. In fact, he created seventy paintings in the last seventy days of his life, an average of one a day—a remarkable pace for such a gifted artist.

Is it healthy to have slimy, sticky, bloodsucking leeches attached to your body?

It can be. Although leeches can't help headaches or mental illnesses (like people in the nineteenth century thought), they are occasionally used in hospitals today to help with blood flow. In one instance, a leech actually helped surgeons reattach a five-year-old boy's ear.

Can a man with one hand get a hit in major league baseball?

Absolutely! Jim Abbott, the one-handed pitcher best known for throwing a no-hitter for the New York Yankees, actually got two hits in his final season in major league baseball. As a matter of fact, Abbott was not the first one-handed baseball player to get a hit. In 1945, Pete Gray got fifty-one hits for the St. Louis Browns. (Gray had lost his right arm in a truck accident when he was a kid, and he had to learn to hit with his left hand.)

CHAPTER 4
Fact and Opinion

What roller coaster reaches speeds of more than 100 miles per hour in less than two seconds?

How long is the world's longest fingernail?

Can a person climb the Empire State Building without any climbing gear?

There is a big difference between fact and opinion. But that doesn't stop some people from telling their opinions as facts or other people from believing opinions as facts. If you can tell the difference between facts and opinions, you will be able to do better on your reading tests. You will also be able to make your spoken and written arguments more convincing.

A **fact** is a statement that is generally accepted to be true and can be checked in and confirmed by several sources. You can find facts in places like textbooks, encyclopedias, or atlases.

An **opinion** is a statement of a personal judgment or a belief that cannot be proven. An opinion is what a person thinks or feels about a subject. It may not be true. Opinions often use the word "most," "best," "worst," or "should." You can find opinions in places like a diary or an editorial, which is an article that tells about one person's opinion.

Fact	Opinion
The New York City subway system runs twenty-four hours a day.	*New York City is the greatest city in the world.*
This statement is a fact because it can be proven. You can prove that the subways run all night long. This is a true statement.	This statement is an opinion because it cannot be proven. You might *think* that it's the greatest city, but there is no way to prove it. This is an opinion.
Congressman Jones voted to decreases sales tax.	*Congressman Jones is the best congressman in the state.*
You can prove this statement by looking at Congressman Jones's voting records. If you can check it, it is a fact.	There is no way to prove this statement. You can prove that Congressman Jones voted to decrease taxes, but it is not possible to prove that someone is the *best* of anything. That is an opinion.

Be alert for statements that sound like facts but are actually opinions. For example, imagine that a friend told you "It is a fact that I am the best basketball player on the team." Your bragging friend is not telling the truth. He or she is just telling you an opinion. Advertisements are often set up to sound like facts, but they are usually opinions.

For more practice, read the passage about Dodonpa on the next page and the sample question that follows.

For Your Amusement

Dodonpa: 0–107 Miles Per Hour in 1.8 Seconds

Last year, I visited Japan with my family. It is a beautiful country with very friendly people. There are mountains that are more than 11,000 feet tall. One of the best parts of the trip was when we visited the Fujikyu Highland Park. They have a roller coaster called Dodonpa. Dodonpa is one of the most incredible roller coasters in the world.

Dodonpa can reach a speed of 107 miles per hour. It also reaches that speed in less than two seconds. That's almost too fast! The roller coaster is 3,900 feet long. Its highest point is more than 170 feet in the air. Even though Dodonpa is not even half the height of the 415-feet-tall "Superman: The Escape" at Six Flags Magic Mountain in California, Dodonpa is faster. And because Dodonpa is faster, it is also more fun!

▶ Write one statement of fact and one statement of opinion from the passage.

Fact: _____

_____

Opinion: _____

_____

Know It All Approach

This question asks you to find a fact and an opinion from the passage. Remember the differences between facts and opinions, as explained in the previous page. Read the passage carefully, and look for good examples of facts and opinions. Underline or circle the examples.

To find a fact, look for a statement that you can prove. Sentences with numbers are often facts. For example, "The roller coaster is 3,900 feet long" is a fact because you can check it. Someone who works at the roller coaster probably knows this is true. "Its highest point is more than 170 feet in the air" could be checked too. You can prove it by measuring the coaster, or, if you don't have time to go to Japan, by confirming it in another source. So it is also a fact.

To find an opinion, look for a statement that tells what someone thinks or feels. If you can't prove it, it is likely an opinion. For example, many people may think that Japan is a beautiful country, but how can you check that? You can't. Some people may think it is a beautiful country. Others may not. Therefore, "It is a beautiful country with very friendly people" is an opinion. So is "Dodonpa is one of the most incredible roller coasters in the world" because you can't prove that something is incredible. That is what the writer thinks, so it is an opinion.

Grosser Than Gross

Fame for a Four-Foot Fingernail

People will do just about anything to get famous. Some of the feats are awe-inspiring. Other feats are just plain silly. But don't tell that to Shridhar Chillal. Chillal is an Indian man who devoted nearly fifty years of his life to growing the world's longest fingernails.

Long fingernails can be cool, but Chillal's fingernails were simply too long. Chillal stopped cutting the fingernails on his left hand when he was fourteen years old, in 1952. They grew and grew and grew for at least fifty years. By the time he got the world record, the combined length of the five fingernails on his left hand measured more than twenty feet. The thumbnail measured 4.8 feet, and the other nails were each at least three feet long.

Chillal's fingernails don't look like regular nails. They're twisted and curled, uneven and irregular. In fact, Chillal's fingernails were not attractive at all. And not only that, but Chillal caused himself physical damage by putting so much extra weight on his hand and by keeping it useless for so long. And the hand is the most important part of the body!

The constant weight of the snake-like nails on Chillal's left hand created pain throughout the left side of his body. His wrist, elbow, and shoulder all hurt him. And because he didn't use his hand for so long, several nerves in his body died. That affected him in many ways, including leaving him deaf in one ear. Chillal's pain also made his job as a news photographer more difficult. That's a shame. Being a photographer is one of the most interesting jobs a person can have.

For nearly half a century, Chillal had to protect his fingernails from being broken. He had to be careful when he slept or ate. He had to be careful when he hugged his grandchildren. He even had to shield his fingernails from strong winds, which could have snapped one of the long nails. He should have spent less time worrying about his nails and more time with his family. World records are nice to have, but it is more important to be healthy.

Directions: Answer questions 1–5 based on the passage about Shridhar Chillal's fingernails.

1. Which statement below is **not** an example of a fact?

   A   Long fingernails can be cool, but Chillal's fingernails were simply too long.
   B   Chillal stopped cutting the fingernails on his left hand when he was fourteen years old.
   C   The combined length of the five fingernails on his left hand measured more than twenty feet.
   D   The thumbnail measured 4.8 feet, and the other nails were each at least three feet long.

2. Which statement below is an example of an opinion?

   A   Because he didn't use his hand for so long, several nerves in his body died.
   B   Chillal caused himself physical damage by putting so much extra weight on his hand.
   C   Chillal's pain also made his job as a news photographer more difficult.
   D   The hand is the most important part of the body.

3. Which sentence from the passage is an example of a fact?

   A   For nearly half a century, Chillal had to protect his fingernails from being broken.
   B   He should have spent less time worrying about his nails and more time with his family.
   C   World records are nice to have.
   D   It is more important to be healthy.

4. Tell why the following sentence is an opinion.

   Being a photographer is one of the most interesting jobs a person can have.

   _____

   _____

5. Explain whether the statement below is a fact or an opinion.

   In fact, Chillal's fingernails were not attractive at all.

   _____

   _____

   _____

Bizarre Human Feats

Alain Robert: The Real Spider-Man

Have you seen the movie *Spider-Man?* It is one of the most exciting movies ever made. The movie is based on a fictitious character. However, there is a real-life Spider-Man who climbs buildings all over the world. His name is Alain Robert. He once even climbed a building dressed as Spider-Man! The daredevil says he shares the same philosophy as the superhero he resembles.

Alain Robert has climbed many of the tallest buildings in the world. Among his achievements are the Sears Tower in Chicago, the Empire State Building in New York City, and the Eiffel Tower in Paris. When Robert climbs these giant structures, he does not use any climbing gear or safety equipment. That is very scary!

In 1998, Robert tried to climb the Petronas Twin Towers in Kuala Lumpur, Malaysia. The Petronas Towers are the tallest office buildings in the world, measuring 1,483 feet tall. It would have been the greatest climbing achievement. But Malaysian police did not let him finish. They captured him as he was at about the sixtieth floor. The police should certainly have let Robert finish his climb.

Today, Alain Robert continues to climb more buildings, acting like Spider-Man. He also continues to break the law by illegally climbing skyscrapers. Someone should change the law so that Alain Robert can scale these buildings.

Directions: Answer questions 6–9 based on the passage about Alain Robert.

6. Which statement below is an opinion from the passage?

   A   *Spider-Man* is one of the most exciting movies ever made.
   B   The police should certainly have let Robert finish his climb.
   C   Alain Robert has climbed many of the tallest buildings in the world.
   D   In 1998, Robert tried to climb the Petronas Twin Towers in Kuala Lumpur, Malaysia.

7. Which statement below is a fact from the passage?

   A   Climbing without climbing gear or safety equipment is very scary!
   B   Alain Robert did not use climbing gear to climb the Eiffel Tower or Sears Tower.
   C   Climbing the Petronas Towers would have been the greatest climbing achievement.
   D   The police should certainly have let Robert finish his climb.

8. Explain how you can tell that the following sentence is an example of a fact.

   The Petronas Towers were the tallest office buildings in the world in 1998, measuring 1,483 feet tall.

   _____

   _____

   _____

9. Which statement below is **not** an example of a fact?

   A   Alain Robert climbed the Sears Tower in Chicago.
   B   The Petronas Towers were the tallest office buildings in the world in 1998, measuring 1,483 feet tall.
   C   Alain Robert climbed the Empire State Building in New York.
   D   Someone should change the law so that Alain Robert can scale these buildings.

Subject Review

Now you have learned the important differences between facts and opinions. Basically, the big difference is that facts can be proven. You can't prove an opinion because every person's opinion is different. As long as you use this knowledge wisely, you'll be able to score extra points on your reading tests.

Knowing the differences between facts and opinions is useful for more reasons than doing well on tests. It's great for arguments and debates. Hopefully you can tell when someone states an opinion but says it is a fact.

For example, if a commercial says, "This is the best video game money can buy," you'll know it's just one person's opinion. Or if your older brother says he is the best-looking person on the planet, you can just tell him it's only his opinion (and it's wrong).

Here are some of the facts asked about at the beginning of this chapter.

What roller coaster reaches speeds more than 100 miles per hour in less than two seconds?
The Dodonpa in Fujikyu Highland Park, Japan, can do this. In fact, its top speed is 107 miles per hour, and it can reach that speed in an astonishing 1.8 seconds.

How long is the world's longest fingernail?
Verrrrrrry long. Shridhar Chillal grew one of his fingernails, the thumbnail on his left hand, to about 4.8 feet. The other nails on the hand were all at least three feet long, making the total length of the nails on his left hand more than twenty feet.

Can a person climb the Empire State Building without any climbing gear?
If you consider Alain Robert a person and not a superhero, then yes, a person can climb some of the world's tallest buildings without support. Robert also climbed the Golden Gate Bridge, the Brooklyn Bridge, and the pyramid-shaped Luxor Hotel in Las Vegas, Nevada.

Outer Space Oddities

Phobos, the Potato Moon of Mars

Earth has one giant, round moon that you can see almost every night. Mars has two moons, Phobos and Deimos, which are much smaller than our moon and not round at all. Their lumpy shapes are elongated so they look like floating potatoes, flying in orbit around the planet Mars. That's how they got their nickname: the potato moons. The two moons are pretty funny looking!

Phobos is the bigger of the two potato moons but is still only about seventeen miles long. That's about the length of the island of Manhattan! Even though Phobos is so *minuscule,* you could see it if you were standing on Mars because Phobos flies very close to the red planet. It also rises and sets three times a day, not just once.

Not only is Phobos very close to Mars but it also is getting closer to the planet by almost one inch every year. That means it will eventually crash into Mars or break up into millions of pieces, creating a ring around Mars. Don't worry, though: This catastrophic event probably won't happen for another 40 to 50 million years. There is still plenty of time to explore Phobos, and maybe even send a person to the tiny moon. (Our own moon is actually getting *farther away* from Earth every year.)

Because Phobos is so small and light, it has very little gravity. The gravity of the tiny Martian moon Phobos is about 1,000 times less than Earth's. That means an astronaut would weigh about three ounces on Phobos. That's less than the weight of this book! In fact, the low gravity would have some amazing effects on humans. A weightlifter would be able to lift a jet airplane. A baseball player could throw a baseball into orbit around the moon. And a high jumper could leap a mile off the surface of Phobos!

Many scientists want to send an astronaut to Phobos. It would be easier to land on Phobos than on Mars, and Phobos could be used as a base to study Mars. The astronaut could also explore its cold surface. It would be amazing if a person walked on the tiny moon one day.

Directions: Answer questions 1–5 about the passage about Phobos.

1. In the second paragraph, what does the word *minuscule* mean?

   A strange
   B tasty
   C small
   D distant

2. Which of the following is an opinion about Phobos?

   A Phobos rises and sets three times a day.
   B An astronaut would weigh about three ounces on Phobos.
   C It would be amazing if a person walked on the tiny moon one day.
   D Phobos is called a "Potato Moon" because it looks like a real potato.

3. What is one similarity between Earth's moon and Mars's moon, Phobos?

   A Both moons will crash into their planets.
   B Both moons are shaped like giant potatoes.
   C Both moons support life in their craters.
   D Both moons orbit their planets.

4. Which statement below is **not** a fact about Phobos?

   A Phobos is only about seventeen miles long.
   B The gravity of Phobos is about 1,000 times less than Earth's.
   C Phobos and Deimos are pretty funny looking!
   D Phobos is getting closer to Mars by almost one inch every year.

5. Write one reason why some scientists want to send an astronaut to Phobos.

   _____

   _____

CHAPTER 5
Summary, Main Idea, and Theme

I'm stuck in quicksand . . . how do I get out?

How long does it take to circle the world alone in a hot-air balloon?

What causes a model volcano to bubble up?

The summary, the main idea, and the theme of a reading selection are all ways of expressing its central idea. It helps to know how summaries, main ideas, and themes are different, as well as how they're similar. Most reading tests will ask you questions that require you to identify the summary, main idea, or theme of a passage.

The **summary** of a passage briefly tells the important information in a passage. It generally describes events in order and includes the most important details. Here is a summary of the passage *Phobos, the Potato Moon of Mars,* that you read on page 43.

> *Phobos is one of Mars's two moons, which are both shaped like lumpy potatoes. Phobos is not very big and doesn't have very strong gravity, so objects would be much lighter there. Scientists want to visit Phobos one day so they can study Mars up close.*

The **main idea** is what a reading selection is *mostly* about. It usually relates to an expositional (informational) passage rather than a narrative (storytelling) one. The author sometimes states the main idea in the first or last few sentences of the first paragraph, and sometimes the title of the passage gives an indication of the main idea. Sometimes the author only suggests the main idea by leaving clues within the passage. A main idea of the passage *Phobos, the Potato Moon of Mars* might be stated as "Phobos is an interesting, potato-shaped moon of Mars."

The **theme** is a more general type of main idea of a passage and is talked about mostly with literary passages like plays, stories, and poems. The theme can be a single word, such as "loneliness" or "friendship," or it can be stated in a phrase like a moral. The theme may not become clear until the end of a passage. For example, the theme in a fable is usually stated at the end of the story. Another way of thinking about theme is to think about what the reader is supposed to learn from a passage. For example, a theme of the story *Cinderella* might be "love conquers all" or "good triumphs over evil."

Turn the page to get sucked into a passage about quicksand.

Quicksand: Not So Quick

Low-budget adventure movies often show people getting sucked into a bottomless pit of quicksand. The hero grabs a branch or a rope to save a life. But it's not true that quicksand is as dangerous as the movies make it seem. Quicksand is just regular sand that has a lot of water in it. Usually that's because water is flowing beneath the sand. Because the sand is so full of water, it can't support the weight of a person's body.

Quicksand will never swallow you into the ground. In fact, sometimes it's not even more than a few feet deep. However, some people panic when they find themselves sinking in soupy sand. As a result, their struggles cause them to sink and possibly drown. If you ever find yourself in quicksand, just relax. If you relax, your body will always float on top of it. If you lie on your back and use slow movements, you can paddle your way to safety. No problem!

▶ What is the main idea of this passage?

A   Heroes in movies often rescue people from quicksand.
B   Quicksand is just regular sand that is filled with water.
C   Quicksand is not as dangerous as the movies make it seem.
D   You should lie on your back and use slow movements so you don't sink in quicksand.

Know It All Approach

Remember that the main idea is what a reading selection is *mostly* about. Be careful not to choose a detail from the passage as its main idea. Try to come up with your own main idea, and then look at the answer choices.

Answer choice (A) lists a detail from the passage about heroes in movies. Is the passage *mostly* about the heroes in movies? It's not, so cross off (A).

Answer choice (B) tells a fact from the passage. It's true, but does it tell the main idea? The passage isn't *mostly* about quicksand being filled with water. So, toss out (B).

Answer choice (C) sounds good. Most of the passage tells how quicksand isn't very dangerous, although it mentions many movies make it seem so. Hold on to (C) and check out (D).

Answer choice (D) tells you a strategy to avoid sinking in quicksand. It's useful, but is it what the passage is *mostly* about? Not really, it's just a detail. (C) is the best answer choice. Pick it!

Sixth Time Is a Charm!

By the end of the 1990s, many achievements in flight were already made. But there was one that eluded adventurers for decades: circling the globe alone in a hot-air balloon. There are many dangers involved, including crashing into the ocean, freezing at the high altitudes, and even getting shot down by hostile countries. That didn't stop Steve Fossett from accomplishing the solo feat in July 2002. Of course, his achievement did not come easy. He failed five times—putting his life in danger several times—before finally getting it right!

Fossett was always driven for adventures. He swam the English Channel, competed in an Alaskan dog sled race, and sailed alone across both the Atlantic and Pacific Oceans. But he had his heart set on becoming the first person to float around the world in a balloon. His first attempt in 1996 barely took him one-tenth of the way across the globe. His second attempt in 1997 carried him halfway across the globe—10,360 miles to be exact—before crash-landing in India.

Fossett's attempt in 1998 took him across Europe, but he was forced to land in Russia. The fourth attempt that Fossett made took him 15,000 miles, but a violent thunderstorm smashed his balloon. His balloon sank more than 29,000 feet through the air, crashing into the shark-infested seas east of Australia. He was rescued by a sailboat.

Fossett's fifth attempt in 2002 ended in South America. He had to survive a night of thunderstorms over the Andes Mountains, and then he ended up landing on a cattle ranch in Brazil.

After all these failures, Fossett was still driven to succeed.

The weather was better for Fossett's sixth attempt, and his balloon flew across the continents at speeds faster than 200 miles per hour. He landed in Australia, having flown around the globe in thirteen days, twelve hours, sixteen minutes, and thirteen seconds at the age of fifty-eight. It just goes to show, if at first you don't succeed, try, try again!

Directions: Answer questions 1–3 based on the passage about Steve Fossett.

1. What is the main idea of this reading selection?

   A   Steve Fossett refused to stop trying to circle the globe in a hot-air balloon.

   B   Steve Fossett had to survive in the shark-infested waters off Australia.

   C   Hot-air balloons are an extremely fun way to travel.

   D   Hot-air balloons are unsafe and should not be used for travel.

2. What is the theme of this reading selection?

   A   procrastination

   B   danger

   C   determination

   D   survival

3. On the lines below, write a summary of the passage about Steve Fossett.

   _____

   _____

   _____

   _____

   _____

 Mad Science

The Lazy Gene

Eugene was a pretty smart kid in school. But despite his talents in the classroom, Gene (as his friends called him) was not very good with getting assignments done on time. Maybe his parents never bought him a calendar, or maybe he was just too lazy to do his homework on time. Whatever the case, the boy had deadline issues. So when he was given two months to prepare his science-fair project, it was no surprise that he waited until the last minute.

Gene figured that he could make a model of a volcano the night before the science fair. It was a relatively simple experiment, he thought, so there was no need to rush. However, when he started to work on his project, the night before the project was due, he began to panic.

A model volcano doesn't require too many ingredients. Your average science-fair volcano is made from six cups flour, two cups salt, four tablespoons cooking oil, red dye, and two cups water, plus baking soda and vinegar. Pretty easy, except for one problem: As Eugene assembled the necessary ingredients, he found, much to his dismay, that he was lacking one of the basics.

Eugene's parents were somehow, impossibly, inexplicably, inconceivably, and completely out of baking soda. Gene knew that baking soda was critical for the project's success. The baking soda and vinegar combine to cause a chemical reaction, which creates carbon dioxide bubbles. (A real volcano also releases carbon dioxide.) It was too late to go to a store, so Gene ended up going to bed knowing that his volcano was missing an important element. He couldn't sleep, though. The concern over his half-finished science project kept him up.

When Eugene got to school, he only had a few minutes until the science fair began. So, he began his frantic search for baking soda. Gene was friendly with the school chef, so he went to the cafeteria and begged for the missing piece. The school's chef felt bad for Gene, who always seemed to be frantically finishing his homework in the morning at the last minute. Fortunately, there was some extra baking soda for Eugene to use. He placed the baking soda into the volcano's crater just as the science fair was about to start.

By the time Eugene's volcano was ready, the science fair had already started. *But at least the project was done,* Gene thought. And when his teacher came by his table, Gene poured the vinegar into his model and waited for the lava to erupt. But it didn't work as well as he had hoped! Eugene had forgotten to put the baking soda in a plastic cup, so the crucial part of the volcano (the baking soda) was all over the place. In fact, Eugene noticed then that his pants were covered in the powder.

Gene's teacher chuckled to herself and moved on to the next project. Later in the week, she gave Eugene his grade for the work: a D! She wrote to Eugene: "You didn't put any effort into your project. You're much too smart to submit such half-hearted work. Next time, try getting someone other than our own cafeteria's chef to give you materials on the very same day of the fair!"

Directions: Answer questions 4–5 based on the passage about Eugene and his volcano.

4. What is the theme to this story?
   A volcanoes
   B preparedness
   C mean teachers
   D baking soda

5. Write a summary of this story on the lines below.

_____

_____

_____

_____

_____

_____

_____

Subject Review

Here is a *summary* of summary, main idea, and theme.

The **summary** lists all of the important details in a passage in chronological order. A summary is usually pretty brief. It should only include the most essential information from the passage.

The **main idea** is what a reading selection is mostly about. The author often states the main idea in the first or last few sentences of the first paragraph.

The **theme** is the moral or main idea of a literary passage. The theme can be a single word, such as "loneliness" or "friendship," or it can be a message, like "A penny saved is a penny earned."

And now you can answer the questions from the start of the chapter.

I'm stuck in quicksand . . . how do I get out?

Well, quicksand is not as dangerous as most folks think. People's bodies are less dense than quicksand, so they actually float on top. It's when people panic and struggle that they can create danger. The best way to escape if you ever find yourself sinking in a murky pool of quicksand is to not panic. Lie down and slowly paddle your way out of trouble.

How long does it take to circle the world alone in a hot-air balloon?

According to Steve Fossett, the only person to accomplish the feat (as of 2003), it takes exactly thirteen days, twelve hours, sixteen minutes, and thirteen seconds. What a crazy way to spend a couple of weeks!

What causes a model volcano to bubble up?

Eugene found it was the combination of baking soda and vinegar. Together, the two elements cause a chemical reaction that creates bubbles of carbon dioxide. (You can even try this at home with an adult's permission.)

CHAPTER 6
Inferences

Why would an entire town wear red, round noses on the same day?

Why does a flying bug turn on and off like a little lamp?

How fast can a person pull an airplane twenty-five meters down a runway?

Reading is like a recipe with two ingredients—words and ideas. Whenever you read something, all kinds of ideas will pop into your head. These ideas—which can include inferences, generalizations, conclusions, and predictions—combine to create a richer understanding of what you read.

Read the following paragraph and learn how each term can apply to it.

> *As she wandered through the department store, Sally was approached by an aggressive "perfume lady" who sprayed her scent on Sally's arm. Sally smelled the perfume and scowled, curling her lips into a frown and shaking her head in disgust. She glared angrily at the woman who sprayed her and then walked off.*

An **inference** is an idea you may have that is based on information in a passage, sometimes combined with stuff you already know. For example, in the above passage, you might infer that Sally can get a little bit mean when someone bothers her.

A **generalization** is an inference about a whole group or category based on information about only a few things in the group or category. For example, you might generalize that Sally doesn't like *any* kind of perfume (the whole perfume category), which might not be true—maybe she just hates this one kind of perfume, but the passage doesn't say.

A **conclusion** is an inference you make using clues and information in a passage. You use information to find a conclusion, much like a detective uses clues to solve a crime. For example, Sally frowned when she smelled the perfume, which might help you conclude that Sally does not like the smell of perfume.

A **prediction** is an inference you make about the future. You use information to figure out what might happen next. For example, because Sally scowled you can predict that Sally will not buy the perfume.

Now the you've sniffed out information about inferences, generalizations, conclusions, and predictions, read the passage on the next page to learn more about inference questions.

For Your Amusement

It was March 14, and everyone in the office was getting ready to celebrate Red Nose Day, a new holiday in Britain and Australia. On Red Nose Day, people raise money for charity while wearing silly red noses and playing games. Most folks in the office were excited to have fun for a day in the name of charity, but not Dave, the office manager.

Dave hated the idea of any occasion getting in the way of work. He refused to wear a silly red nose or participate in the festival's games. In fact, he even told other workers to avoid all the wackiness. Dave was just about to criticize one of his coworkers for being noisy when Rob crept up behind him. Wearing a giant red nose and a massive red wig, Rob smacked Dave in the face with a pie! Stunned, Dave stared at Rob, unblinking and unmoving, with pie dripping off his reddening face.

▶ Which of the following will most likely happen next?

A Dave will ask his coworkers to be quiet.
B Rob will take off his red nose.
C Dave will give Rob a good scolding.
D Rob will make a donation to charity.

Know It All Approach

This multiple-choice question asks you to make a prediction. That means you should use information to make an inference about the future. Use clues to decide what most likely will happen next.

Dave doesn't like the British holiday Red Nose Day. Rob, however, gets carried away with it. You can conclude that Dave hates Red Nose Day, and Rob loves it. When Dave gets hit with a pie, you can conclude that he is very angry because he stares at Rob and turns red. Make up your own prediction, and then check the answer choices.

If Dave is really upset, will he ask his coworkers to be quiet? Maybe, so hold onto answer choice (A) and try (B). Will Rob take off his nose? There is no reason to predict that, so cross off (B). But there is reason to believe that Dave will scold Rob, answer choice (C). In fact, it is *more* likely that Dave will scold Rob than it is that Dave will ask his coworkers to be quiet. So (C) is a better answer choice than (A). Again, there are no clues that tell you Rob will make a donation, so you can also cross of answer choice (D). Answer choice (C) is the best answer choice.

Zenon and the Fireflies

"What was that?" Zenon, my little brother, whispered urgently, grabbing my arm. Zenon was scared of his own shadow sometimes. Now, hiking out in the woods together, he seemed downright terrified.

At first I didn't know what he was talking about, so I assumed his overactive imagination was acting up, like it often did. But Zenon definitely seemed more worried than usual. "There it is again!" he shrieked, pointing to his right in the darkness.

This time, I saw what he saw: a quick flash of light maybe twenty-five feet away from us, between two trees. Nobody was out here with us, so the bright light didn't make sense. Then, before I could speak, another flash of light flickered just to our left. Zenon threw his arms around me and started to whimper.

At that moment, a little one-inch-long bug flew past my face, momentarily lighting its back brightly.

"Hey! It's a firefly!" I told Zenon. "We've got nothing to worry about, little bro!"

Zenon's fear turned to curiosity. "Why do they glow?" he asked.

Because I had just written a report about them, I knew the answer: "It's how they communicate with each other," I told him. "Some people think it's also to warn other animals that they aren't tasty. That doesn't stop frogs, though; some frogs eat enough of them that they actually glow too!"

A relieved Zenon chuckled at the thought. "Do you think we can try to catch some?" he asked, without a hint of fear in his voice. I smiled.

Directions: Answer questions 1–4 based on the passage about Zenon and the fireflies.

1. Why did Zenon become less scared?

    _____

    _____

2. What can you conclude about the narrator of the story?

    A   She is terrified of fireflies.
    B   She doesn't like her little brother.
    C   She knows some facts about fireflies.
    D   She loves her parents very much.

3. What do you think will happen next in this story?

    _____

    _____

4. Which of these statements is a generalization that can be made from the story?

    A   Frogs eat all sorts of insects.
    B   The firefly uses its glow to warn other animals.
    C   Older sisters are afraid of insects.
    D   Zenon wants to catch fireflies.

Bizarre Human Feats

Just Yoking

"I cannot believe that we are watching a man *pull an airplane* using his own strength," Trey whispered to Nate. "It's not like he's pulling a small plane either. He's pulling a Boeing 737 jet airplane across the runway! Those giant jets can hold more than 100 passengers!"

Nate smiled and added, "Yeah, but there are bigger airplanes than a 737. It's really not that impressive."

Together, Trey and Nate watched the mammoth Norwegian man pull the aircraft along the runway. According to the rules of the annual World's Strongest Man competition, a contestant has to pull the plane twenty-five meters to qualify for the race. It's just one of the many contests the athletes must endure. The giant man pulled the 737 the required distance in less than forty-four seconds, and then collapsed from exhaustion. "What a wimp!" Nate cried.

Nate and Trey next headed to the weightlifting contest called the Yoke. That's where the athletes have to balance about 600 pounds on a bar on their shoulders and walk as far as they can. Two equal weights hang on both ends of the bar.

"The Yoke is easy," Nate said to his friend. "I could do it if I wanted to. I just don't feel like it today. Look at that guy's muscles," Nate said, pointing to a stout, thick, bulging blond man struggling to shuffle his feet with more than a quarter-ton of weight on his back. "They're not that big."

Trey didn't respond to his friend's outrageous claims. He was too busy looking at his own muscles. "I'd like to enter the World's Strongest Man competition someday," he muttered to himself. Trey flexed his biceps and wondered how much work he'd need to do to be able to pull a plane.

"You?" Nate joked. "You couldn't drag a wagon full of tennis balls, let alone an *airplane*!"

Trey ignored Nate's comments, as usual. Instead, he started to think about how he could become the World's Strongest Man when he got older. He flexed his muscles again and pulled in his gut, and he felt a sudden urge to start working out.

Directions: Answer questions 5–7 based on the passage about Trey, Nate, and the World's Strongest Man competition.

5. What is one conclusion you can draw about the World's Strongest Man competition?

   _____

   _____

6. What can you infer about Nate from the passage?

   A Nate appreciates how hard the athletes work.
   B Nate is arrogant and even a bit cruel.
   C Nate wants to train to be an athlete.
   D Nate is the world's strongest man.

7. What do you predict Trey will do after the competition is over?

   A He will play table tennis.
   D He will make himself a sandwich.
   C He will work out in a gym.
   D He will take a nap.

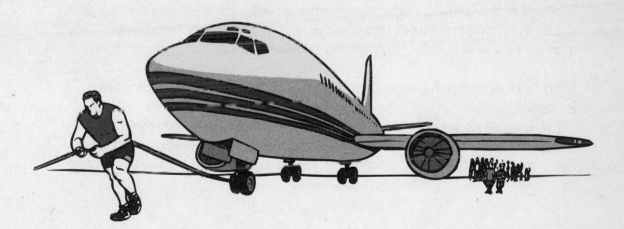

Subject Review

Can you fit all of this into your *Know It All* brain? Check the definitions below, just to be sure you understand them.

An **inference** is an idea or thought based on information. You can make an inference by making an educated guess using what you already know.

A **generalization** is a general inference that is not specific.

A **conclusion** is a decision you make using clues in a story. You use information to find a conclusion, much like a detective uses clues to solve a crime.

A **prediction** is an inference you make about the future. You use clues to figure out what will happen next.

Now, back to those questions from the start of this chapter.

Why would an entire town wear red, round noses on the same day?
Red Nose Day is a new British/Australian holiday, during which people wear red noses and try to raise money for charity. The event also features games, auctions, and other fun stuff.

Why does a flying bug turn on and off like a little lamp?
Fireflies use their glowing abilities to communicate with each other. Some people think it's also to warn other animals that they aren't tasty. That doesn't stop frogs though. Some frogs eat enough of them that they actually glow too!

How fast can a person pull an airplane twenty-five meters down a runway?
The Norwegian athlete whom Trey and Nate saw pulled a plane twenty-five meters in about forty-four seconds. But some athletes can accomplish the mighty feat in fewer than forty seconds. The fastest time in the 1999 World's Strongest Man championships was 39.48 seconds.

CHAPTER 7
Genre and Purpose

Why would anyone write about a farting dog?

Who was the first American woman to win three gold medals in a single Olympics?

Why does an article about a smelly ten-foot-tall flower exist?

I s your brain ready to take over the world yet? Well, it just might be after you complete this chapter about the genre and purpose of a reading selection. The definitions are below.

Genre is a category that describes the style and content of a text. *Know It All!* is a workbook, which is very different than a newspaper, which is very different than a poem, which is very different than other genres.

The following is a description of different genres. Your brain is going to plump when you read these!

A **novel** is a lengthy work of fiction, often with a complex plot and cast of characters.

A **short story** is a short work of fiction, often with a specific, simple plot and only a few characters.

A **reference book** contains factual information about one subject or a variety of subjects.

A **biography** tells factual information about the life of a real person.

A **play** is usually a work of fiction dramatically performed on a stage by actors.

A **poem** can be fictional or factual and is written with line breaks, rhyme, and rhythm, and sometimes without full sentences.

Texts are written for many different reasons and many different **purposes.** Some texts are written to be entertaining, some are written to be informative, and some are written to be persuasive. Sometimes an author will write a text to entertain, inform, and persuade at the same time!

Examples of texts that can **inform** readers are biographies, informative articles, and reference books. Examples of texts that can **entertain** readers are short stories, plays, poems, and novels. Examples of texts that can **persuade** readers are editorials in newspapers, advertisements, and persuasive essays.

What is the purpose of *Know It All!*? Well, all three! *Know It All!* is here to inform you and entertain you—giving you facts that are true and fascinating! And *Know It All!* is also here to persuade you—you *can* know it all, you *can* know it all, you *can* know it all . . . .

 **Grosser Than Gross**

Blame the Bacteria

Do you (a) pretend you don't smell anything, (b) blame it on the dog, or (c) make a big deal of the smell? Yes, this is referring to farts, toots, cuttin' the cheese—whatever you call them.

Certain foods cause farts. You may even know the infamous bean song: "Eat your beans. They're good for your heart. The more you eat, the more you fart." Have you ever wondered why beans, cabbage, peas, and other foods make you gassy?

Beans and many other gas-causing foods contain a sugar called oligosaccharide. The molecules are enormous, and humans lack a certain enzyme so the small intestine is unable to absorb them. Instead, the larger molecules move into the large intestine where bacteria attack them. Because oligosaccharides are not digested in the small intestine, there are lots of them for the bacteria to eat. The more the bacteria eat, the more gas the bacteria release. So the next time something smelly wafts through the air, don't blame the dog. Blame the bacteria.

▶ Which was **most likely** the author's purpose for writing this article?

A   to list all of the different types of foods that cause gas
B   to persuade readers about the tastiness of beans
C   to inform readers about how certain foods cause gas
D   to describe the author's personal experiences with farting

Know It All Approach

Did the author write the article to list the types of foods that cause gas? Although the author lists these foods, the passage is mainly about how gas is produced. So, answer choice (A) is not correct. Draw a line through it. Did the author write the article to persuade readers about the tastiness of beans? Look in the article for information about the tastiness of beans. There isn't any! That means answer choice (B) is wrong. Cross it off! Did the author write the article to inform readers about how certain foods cause gas? There is lots of information in the article about how certain foods cause gas. This is probably correct, but check (D) just in case. The author didn't describe any personal experiences, so answer choice (D) is not correct. Answer choice (C) is correct.

Extreme Sports

Go, Go, Go!

The runner Wilma Rudolph has always fascinated me. As a little girl, Wilma Rudolph was probably the slowest of all her twenty-one brothers and sisters. Why? Because Wilma Rudolph's left leg was paralyzed when she was very young as a result of polio, a disease that affects the muscles and nerves.

Doctors said that Rudolph would never be able to walk. That didn't stop Rudolph's family from working hard to help her. Doctors suggested that massaging her legs might eventually help her, so Rudolph's brothers and sisters would massage her legs every day—sometimes four times a day! By the time she was eight years old, Rudolph was able to walk with a leg brace. And three years later, she could walk without the leg brace. Those leg rubs must have really worked!

If I were Rudolph, I probably would have been happy just being able to walk without a brace. But Rudolph was not satisfied with just being able to walk. She decided she wanted to become an athlete!

Wilma Rudolph became a star sprinter and basketball player in high school before becoming one of the nation's best track-and-field athletes. When she was only sixteen, she was a member of the relay race team that won the bronze medal at the Olympic Games in Melbourne, Australia. Four years later, she set a world record for the 100-meter dash, although some people discredit that because of the high wind speeds that day. At the 1960 Olympic Games in Rome, Italy, Rudolph won three gold medals. She was the first American woman to win three gold medals in a single Olympics.

I recently watched a biography of Rudolph on television that showed her running in the 1960 Olympics. I knew the race had already happened and that she won. But as I watched her race around the track, I couldn't help but shout, "Go, go, go!"

Directions: Answer questions 1–3 based on the passage about Wilma Rudolph.

1. Which of the following was most likely the author's purpose for writing *Go, Go, Go!*?

    A   to prove that leg rubs always heal people suffering from polio

    B   to share an entertaining story about the Olympics

    C   to compare what doctors believed about Rudolph with what her family believed

    D   to teach readers about Rudolph's challenges and successes

2. Which of the following would **most likely** contain more information about Wilma Rudolph's life?

    A   *A Guide to Track and Field*

    B   *A Biography of Wilma Rudolph*

    C   *The Mystery at the Olympics*

    D   *Poems Celebrating Athletes*

3. From which book might the article *Go, Go, Go!* have been taken?

    A   *A Guide to the Roman Olympic Games*

    B   *The Farmer's Almanac*

    C   *My Inspirational Stories of Athletes*

    D   *High School Basketball Stars*

Grosser Than Gross

The Smelliest Flower

People often give flowers to friends and family for birthdays and other special events. But hopefully they don't give their friends a flower called *titan arum*. The *titan arum* is a giant flower that smells like spoiled, rotting meat! In fact, most people refer to it by its gross nickname, "the corpse flower." Its putrid odor is so strong that people can smell it from pretty far away.

A Rotten Bloom

Scientists think that the flower's awful smell is designed to attract insects—specifically, dung beetles and sweat bees. Those insects help pollinate the plant so it can reproduce. The plant doesn't always smell badly, though. It only emits its horrible scent when it is in bloom. Blooms can last a few days and usually happen just a few times in the plant's forty-year life. The corpse flower also smells worst at night during its bloom.

Smell and Size

Not only is the *titan arum* the world's worst-smelling flower, but it is also the world's biggest flower. One corpse flower was measured at around ten feet tall! That's taller than the tallest person who ever lived! Corpse flowers can also weigh up to 170 pounds.

Popular Fragrance

Even though the corpse flower stinks so terribly, people have always wanted to see and smell the plant in person. When a blooming *titan arum* was on display in London in the 1930s, police had to control the crowd! When a corpse flower was on display in California in 1999, 76,000 people came to suffer the flower's stench.

Another reason that people like to see and smell the *titan arum* is because it is so rare. The *titan arum* originally came from the rainforests of Sumatra, a small island in Southeast Asia. Now, it is possible to see them bloom on rare occasion in the United States. Maybe you will be lucky enough to see one someday. Or perhaps you will be unlucky enough to smell one!

Directions: Answer questions 4–8 based on the passage about the smelliest flower.

4. The author probably divided the article into sections in order to

   A emphasize different types of details about the *titan arum.*
   B convince readers that the paragraph about size is more interesting than the paragraph about fragrance.
   C list each step in the corpse flower's blooming process in order.
   D amuse readers by providing funny titles for each section.

5. Why does the author compare the smell of the *titan arum* to spoiled, rotting meat?

   A to persuade readers that flowers are like meat
   B to entertain readers with funny comparisons
   C to help readers understand the facts about the *titan arum*
   D to make readers believe everything the author writes about the *titan arum*

6. Describe the purpose of the article *The Smelliest Flower.* Support your answer with details from the article.

   _____

   _____

   _____

   _____

7. From which of the following was the article *The Smelliest Flower* probably taken?

   A a reference book
   B a short story
   C a biography
   D a novel

8. Which of the following would **most likely** contain more information about the pollination and blooming of the *titan arum*?

   A *Petal by Petal: Short Stories about Fragrant Flowers*
   B *How to Plant and Raise a Successful Garden*
   C *The Day the Air Stank: My Experiences Visiting the Corpse Flower*
   D *1,001 Things You Need to Know about the Corpse Flower*

Subject Review

Phew! This chapter has been awe-inspiring, educational, and incredibly smelly. It was also full of information. You learned about the different types of genres and the reasons why they're written. See below for a quick review, and then the answers to the questions on page 61.

A **novel** is a lengthy work of fiction, often with a complex plot and cast of characters.

A **short story** is a short work of fiction, often with a specific, simple plot and only a few characters.

A **reference book** contains factual information about a wide variety of subjects.

A **biography** contains factual information about the life of a real person.

A **play** is usually a work of fiction (sometimes nonfiction) performed on a stage by actors.

A **poem** is a style of writing written with line breaks, rhyme, and rhythm, and usually without full sentences.

The three main purposes of writing are to **inform, entertain,** or **persuade** readers.

Why would anyone write about a farting dog?
The writer was giving information about farts. It fit the passage. And maybe the author had a weird sense of humor.

Who was the first American woman to win three gold medals in a single Olympics?
That would be Wilma Rudolph. Her story is particularly amazing because her left leg was paralyzed when she was very young. Rudolph's family helped her to walk, and eventually she became the fastest woman in the world!

Why does an article about a smelly ten-foot-tall flower exist?
Because someone, somewhere, sometime pinched his or her nose tightly, looked closely at the flower to study it, and wrote everything down that they could so that people could learn about it! The author wanted to inform and entertain the reader.

Bizarre Human Feats

The Last Straw

Linda walked into the kitchen and nearly fell over. Her brother Michael was sitting at the kitchen table with what looked like 100 drinking straws stuffed into his mouth. His cheeks were puffed out from all the straws in his mouth, and his lips were expanded to maximum capacity. Michael reached for another straw from the box in front of him and slipped it into his already overcrowded mouth.

"What are you doing?" shrieked Linda.

"Mphfmfg," replied Michael. He pointed to an open book on the floor, showing a picture of a man with 210 drinking straws jammed into his mouth. The man in the picture was a Swiss gentleman named Marco Hort, and he had set the record for the most straws held in the mouth. Apparently, Michael was trying to beat Marco's record.

"Oh my!" Linda said. "You're going to hurt yourself! You'd better take those straws out of your mouth before you choke!"

"Bmpgh hmphrm!" Michael replied, pointing again to the picture in the book.

Linda looked at her brother. "What you're doing is dangerous," she said firmly. "I care about you and don't want to see you harm yourself. Please take the straws out of your mouth," she begged him, starting to sound worried.

Michael thought for a moment about what his sister said, and then he slowly started to take the straws out of his mouth. One by one, he pulled them out of his mouth and put the used straws back into the box of straws on the table.

Directions: Answer questions 1–4 based on the passage on the previous page.

1. Why did Michael take the straws out of his mouth?

   A   Linda took the straws out of his mouth.
   B   The straws were beginning to hurt his face.
   C   Michael did not want to upset his sister.
   D   The world record was too difficult to beat.

2. To what genre does this passage **most likely** belong?

   A   reference book
   B   short story
   C   poem
   D   autobiography

3. What is the **most likely** purpose of this passage?

   A   to persuade readers
   B   to teach readers
   C   to inform readers
   D   to entertain readers

4. Write a sentence that tells the main idea of this passage.

   _____

   _____

CHAPTER 8
Comparing and Contrasting

What three brothers
all played major league
baseball during the 1940s?

What would life be like
if you lived on Venus?

What lazy animal sleeps
up to twenty hours a day?

Comparing and contrasting information in a passage or passages can help you learn about similarities and differences between the people, places, and ideas you are reading about. When you are writing the answer to an open-response question, comparing and contrasting is a great tool to show that you understand everything you have read.

As Similar as Peas in a Pod

When you **compare,** you figure out how two or more things are alike. For example, apples and oranges are alike because they are both kinds of fruits. They are also alike because they are both healthy food choices.

As Different as Night and Day

When you **contrast,** you figure out how two or more things are different. For example, apples and oranges are different because apples are hard and crunchy, and oranges are soft and juicy. They are also different because apples are green, yellow, or red, whereas oranges are, well, orange.

On a test, compare-and-contrast questions may ask you to find similarities or differences between the settings, characteristics, characters, details, or other elements of a passage or of two or more separate passages.

Some compare-and-contrast questions will ask you only to compare. Some questions will ask you only to contrast. Some compare-and-contrast questions will require you to write about both differences and similarities in your own words. For these open-response compare-and-contrast questions, always support your answers with information from the passage(s).

 **Extreme Sports**

Baseball Brothers

Even many people who don't like sports have heard the name Joe DiMaggio. He was a famous baseball player who played for thirteen seasons for the New York Yankees, and he set a record by getting a hit in each of fifty-six consecutive games. Joe DiMaggio had a younger brother, Dom, who was not as famous but also a very good baseball player. Dom DiMaggio played for eleven seasons for the Boston Red Sox. Dom got a hit in each of thirty-four consecutive games. Both Dom and Joe DiMaggio played outfield, and they even played outfield together on the same All-Star team!

Another brother, Vince, was not as good a hitter as either of his brothers. In fact, Vince DiMaggio struck out more than anybody else in the National League in six seasons! Vince played from 1937–1946. Only Joe made the Baseball Hall of Fame.

▶ Write one similarity and one difference between Joe and Dom DiMaggio.

_____

_____

Know It All Approach

Read the passage and question carefully. Make sure you know exactly what it's asking for. If you misread it, you might only write one similarity or one difference. You have to write *one of each*!

Think about your answer, and use information from the passage. What's different between Joe and Dom? Use facts to support your answer. Plan how you want to write your answer with these facts. For example, if you want to say that both brothers played outfield, but they played for different teams, your answer could look like the following:

One similarity between Dom and Joe DiMaggio is that they played outfield. A difference

between them is that Dom played for the Red Sox while Joe played for the Yankees.

Make sure you write your answer neatly in complete sentences, and then revise it before you move on to the next question.

Outer Space Oddities

Venus: Our (Evil?) Twin Planet

After the Sun and the Moon, the planet Venus is the brightest object in the sky (besides, of course, low-flying airplanes). However, you can only see Venus in the early morning or the early evening, near dawn and dusk. That's because Venus's orbit is closer to the Sun than Earth's orbit. So, we can only see Venus when Earth is rotated toward the Sun and only when the Sun is not so bright that it takes over the sky.

For centuries, scientists considered Venus as Earth's "Sister Planet" because it seemed so similar. But before you laugh, realize that those scientists were partly correct. Venus and Earth are alike in a number of ways. But they also have remarkable differences.

No two planets have closer orbits than Venus and Earth. In fact, the planets' orbits are only about forty million kilometers apart at the closest point—that's practically down the street in the interstellar neighborhood. Also, the two planets are almost exactly the same size. Earth is barely 5 percent bigger. On a scale model, Venus and Earth look identical. They both have clouds in the atmosphere, lightning storms, and a few craters on their surfaces. But before you start packing your bags to move to Venus, you should know that the similarities end there.

The average temperature on Earth is a fairly comfortable 60 degrees Fahrenheit. On Venus you would need a rather powerful air conditioner. Its average temperature is a scalding 880 degrees Fahrenheit! That intense heat guarantees that the planet has no liquid water, including oceans, and is unable to support human life.

The element of Earth's atmosphere that allows animals to breathe is oxygen. Venus has none. Instead, Venus has a lot of carbon dioxide, which is poisonous to humans. In addition, on Earth it rains water, but scientists believe that the rain on Venus likely contains deadly sulfuric acid!

Even if you could somehow deal with the heat, the carbon dioxide, the lack of water, and the acid rain, you still couldn't live on Venus. That's because the pressure on the surface of the planet is too intense for human bodies. You would be crushed by the heaviness of the air—just like a scuba diver who dives too deep can be crushed by the weight of the water.

While many scientists still consider the moonless Venus our "Sister Planet," it is more like an irritated and unfriendly older sibling than an identical twin.

Directions: Answer questions 1–4 about Venus, our twin sister.

1. Which of the following is a similarity between Venus and Earth?

   A You can scuba dive on both planets.
   B Both are very bright in the sky.
   C Earth and Venus have clouds.
   D Both planets have many craters.

2. What is **not** a difference between Venus and Earth?

   A lightning storms
   B liquid oceans
   C an oxygen atmosphere
   D a comfortable temperature

3. Write one similarity between Earth's and Venus's physical characteristics.

   _____

   _____

4. Write one difference between Earth's and Venus's atmospheres.

   _____

   _____

Alternative Animals

Koalas versus Penguins

If you walk along the shores of southeastern Australia, you are likely to find two of Australia's cutest and most cherished animals—koalas and penguins—living extraordinarily different lives. Koalas live in the trees and enjoy relatively peaceful lives. Penguins spend most of their day in the water, living hectic, frenzied, and very difficult lives.

Koalas eat mainly the leaves of eucalyptus trees. The leaves don't have a lot of calories, so the koala bears conserve energy by sleeping—a lot. In fact, they sleep up to twenty hours a day. That means they're only awake for a few hours per day! Because they are nocturnal animals, koalas are most active at night. That makes them seem even more lazy to people because we usually only see them during the day (when they're sleeping in the trees).

Koalas are lucky, too—they have few natural predators (animals that eat them). However, people have killed koalas for their fur and have also taken over their land for human purposes.

While the koalas are dozing away in their trees, the penguins are working hard just to survive. Most of them have to spend a lot of time in the sea trying to catch fish or squid for food. They also have to catch fish to feed their babies. And when the penguins are in the water, they'd better watch out for seals and killer whales! Penguins are yummy treats to those creatures. Sadly, people pose a great danger to penguins. Penguins often die from the trash and oil spills at sea, and cars frequently kill them on land.

Most penguins are also nocturnal, so they sleep during the day. Unfortunately, their hectic schedule means that they don't have too much time to sleep. Sometimes they even have to catch a nap while floating on their back at sea. Those poor penguins!

So while both koalas and penguins live in Australia—sometimes side by side—they live in very different ways. Just ask a koala—if you can wake one!

Directions: Answer questions 5–8 about koalas and penguins.

5. What is a similarity between koalas and penguins?

   A   Koalas and penguins both live in trees.
   B   Koalas and penguins are both eaten by seals.
   C   Koalas and penguins both eat squid.
   D   Koalas and penguins are both nocturnal.

6. How are the diets of penguins and koalas different?

   A   The penguin's diet is more varied.
   B   The penguin's diet is all vegetarian.
   C   The koala's diet is difficult to catch.
   D   The koala's diet is high in calories.

7. What is one similarity between the environments where penguins and koalas live?

   _____

   _____

8. Write one difference between the daily lives of penguins and koalas

   _____

   _____

Subject Review

By now, you've seen how comparing and contrasting can be useful to show how two things are alike or different. You've also seen the many ways that you might be tested on the skill.

Compare-and-contrast questions, as you've seen, can be multiple choice or open response. You will have to support your open-response questions from information in the passage.

And now you can answer the questions from the beginning of the chapter.

What three brothers all played major league baseball during the 1940s?

Joe, Dom, and Vince DiMaggio all played major league baseball together in the 1940s. Joe, a Yankee, was the best hitter of the three of them. Dom was very good and played for the Red Sox. Vince, the oldest, struck out a lot of times.

What would life be like if you lived on Venus?

You wouldn't be able to live there. Venus would be unbearably hot—hot enough to melt lead! The air on Venus is so heavy that your body would be crushed, and the air is poisonous, so it wouldn't be a great place to live at all.

What lazy animal sleeps up to twenty hours a day?

That would be the Australian native, the koala. And don't call it a koala *bear,* either. The koala may look like a cute, cuddly bear, but it is not a bear. It's considered to be a type of animal called a marsupial. It sleeps a lot so it doesn't waste any energy. But it also sleeps a lot because it doesn't worry about much. It has few natural predators, so it doesn't spend much time running around. (Unfortunately, it does have to worry about human's influence on their habitat and livelihood.)

CHAPTER 9
Poetry

What poem was used to name a professional NFL football team?

How can a fuzzy little groundhog predict the weather?

Which former president was shot in the chest but continued to deliver a speech?

If you want to inspire your brain, pump it up with some poetry. Poetry is full of images of natural beauty, the pain of love lost, epic tales of heroism, and humor—all the things that make life interesting. Also, understanding the basics of poetry can help you do well in school and on reading tests.

So to begin inspiring your *Know It All* brain, learn the following terms. These are literary devices that are often used in poems, and you'll likely be tested on them.

Alliteration is the repetition of sounds at the beginning of words and stressed syllables. A little alliteration can change plain prose into powerful poetry.

Meter is a regular pattern of stressed and unstressed syllables. Different meters can affect the speed and tone of a poem.

Rhyme is the repetition of sounds at the ends of words. Usually the rhyme in a poem comes at the end of the lines. Sometimes the rhyme appears in the middle of the lines. This is called *internal rhyme.*

Free verse is a type of poetry that does not have regular meter or does not follow a rhyme pattern.

Imagery is language that appeals to the senses and helps the reader to imagine the look, sound, touch, smell, and taste of what is being described.

Onomatopoeia is the use of words that imitate sounds, such as "buzz," "hiss," and "hoot."

A **stanza** is a grouping of lines within a poem. Sometimes each stanza of a poem has the same number of lines.

 **Art-rageous**

Poe the Poet

Did you know that Edgar Allen Poe wrote poems as well as short stories? Hey, you can't spell "poem" without "Poe." One of Poe's poems was so amazing that it inspired the name of a NFL football team. It's true. The Superbowl XXXV champions, the Baltimore Ravens, was named after Edgar Allen Poe's famous poem, "The Raven." Poe lived in Baltimore for a number of years and is now buried in a Baltimore church cemetery. The city wanted to honor him in 1996 by naming their football team after him.

Here is the first stanza of Edgar Allen Poe's "The Raven":

Once upon a midnight dreary, while I pondered, weak and weary,
Over many a quaint and curious volume of forgotten lore,
While I nodded, nearly napping, suddenly there came a tapping,
As of some one gently rapping, rapping at my chamber door.
"Tis some visitor," I muttered, "tapping at my chamber door —
Only this and nothing more."

▶ Which of the following contains alliteration from the poem?

A   Once upon a midnight dreary,
B   While I nodded, nearly napping,
C   tapping at my chamber door
D   Only this and nothing more.

Know It All Approach

You need to remember what alliteration means to answer this question. That's why it's so important to familiarize yourself with the terms from page 80. Alliteration is the repeated sound at the beginning of words. The first two lines of "The Raven" contain alliteration. "Weak and weary" and "quaint and curious" are both examples.

Read the sentences in the answer choices, paying special attention to words that start with the same sound. In answer choice (A), there is no common starting sound. Cross it off. In answer choice (B), the words "nodded, nearly napping" start with the same sound, so it seems correct. Check answer choices (C) and (D) to be sure. Neither answer choice includes alliteration, so answer choice (B) is correct.

WILD CARDS

You may know the importance of February 2 from the hilarious Bill Murray movie, *Groundhog Day*. But the origins of Groundhog Day actually date back to the Middle Ages. People believed that an animal waking up from hibernation could foretell the future of the winter. If the animal saw its own shadow, it was scared into running back into its hole for six more weeks of winter. If the day was cloudy and there was no shadow, an early spring was predicted. Germans brought the tradition to America from Europe. Since 1887, Groundhog Day celebrations have been centered in Punxsutawney, Pennsylvania. That's where tens of thousands of spectators gather each February 2 to see whether the groundhog named Phil will see his shadow. But shadows can be hard to keep track of, or so says the poem "My Shadow" by Robert Louis Stevenson.

My Shadow
by Robert Louis Stevenson

I have a little shadow that goes in and out with me,
And what can be the use of him is more than I can see.
He is very, very like me from the heels up to the head;
And I see him jump before me, when I jump into my bed.

The funniest thing about him is the way he likes to grow—
Not at all like proper children, which is always very slow;
For he sometimes shoots up taller like an India-rubber ball,
And he sometimes gets so little that there's none of him at all.

He hasn't got a notion of how children ought to play,
And can only make a fool of me in every sort of way.
He stays so close beside me, he's a coward you can see;
I'd think shame to stick to nursie as that shadow sticks to me!

One morning, very early, before the sun was up,
I rose and found the shining dew on every buttercup;
But my lazy little shadow, like an arrant sleepy-head,
Had stayed at home behind me and was fast asleep in bed.

Directions: Answer questions 1–4 based on Robert Louis Stevenson's poem.

1. How many stanzas are there in "My Shadow"?

   A   1
   B   2
   C   3
   D   4

2. Which words in the first stanza rhyme?

   A   *me* and *head*
   D   *me* and *see*
   C   *me* and *bed*
   D   *see* and *bed*

3. Which of the following poetic devices is used in this poem?

   A   alliteration
   B   onomatopoeia
   C   meter
   D   internal rhyme

4. Is this poem an example of free verse? Explain why or why not.

   _____

   _____

   _____

Teddy Roosevelt's Fateful Eve

October 14 of Nineteen-Twelve—a fateful eve
Saved by luck that you would not believe.
A single man was saved that day,
A former president of the U.S. of A.

The candidate was stumping for votes
By delivering a speech from his notes.
Theodore Roosevelt was the man's name,
And toward him an assassin would take aim.

Bang! a bullet fired straight toward Teddy's heart
Before his speech could even start.
A madman had lifted and fired his gun.
But Teddy, rugged and robust, would not be undone.

The bullet struck the president right in his chest,
But the big man must have been blessed.
Mr. Roosevelt continued to wave his arm
For the bullet had barely caused any harm.

The notes of his speech in Roosevelt's breast pocket
Helped to slow down the .32 rocket.
And while his white vest was bloodied and torn,
The damage was not more than a rose's thorn.

Unfazed, Roosevelt delivered his address
Of change and improvement; he did not digress.
And to his assassin did Teddy decree,
"It will take much more than that to kill me!"

Directions: Answer questions 5–8 based on the poem about Teddy Roosevelt.

5. Which line from the poem gives an example of onomatopoeia?

   A   Bang! a bullet fired straight toward Teddy Roosevelt's heart
   B   And while his white vest was bloodied and torn
   C   Of change and improvement and of progress
   D   "It will take much more than that to kill me!"

6. Which line from the poem gives an example of alliteration?

   A   A stroke of luck that you wouldn't believe
   B   Yet an assassin would take deadly aim
   C   But Teddy, rugged and robust, would not be undone
   D   Helped to slow down the .32 rocket

7. How many stanzas are in the poem?

   A   3
   B   4
   C   5
   D   6

8. Which poetic device is **not** used in this poem?

   A   rhyme
   B   free verse
   C   meter
   D   alliteration

Subject Review

Ah, poetry. No English class—or life—would be complete without it. So, refresh your memory by reviewing these important terms.

Alliteration is the repetition of sounds at the beginning of words and stressed syllables.

Meter is a regular pattern of stressed and unstressed syllables.

Rhyme is the repetition of sounds at the ends of words.

Free verse is a type of poetry that does not have regular meter or does not follow a rhyme pattern.

Imagery is language that appeals to the senses and helps describe the look, sound, touch, smell, and taste of what is being described.

Onomatopoeia is the use of words that imitate sounds such as "buzz," "hiss," and "hoot."

A **stanza** is a grouping of lines within a poem.

What poem was used to name a professional NFL football team?

The Baltimore Ravens is named after the Edgar Allen Poe poem, "The Raven." The Ravens went on to win Superbowl XXXV in January 2001.

How can a fuzzy little groundhog predict the weather?

The legend is that if a groundhog sees its shadow on February 2, then there will be six more weeks of winter. If the day is cloudy and there is no shadow, then there will be an early spring. Whether the groundhog is accurate is another story. Some people say he is accurate only about 40 percent of the time!

Which former president was shot in the chest but continued to deliver a speech?

Teddy Roosevelt was nicknamed the Rough Rider in part because of his rough and tough character. He proved that character one day when he was shot from close range before giving a speech. The bullet hit his vest pocket, where the speech was stored, and Roosevelt only suffered a minor flesh wound. He went on to deliver the speech anyway!

CHAPTER 10
Literary Techniques

What did the man who
invented dynamite do to
promote peace?

Who convinced
Thomas Jefferson
to write the Declaration
of Independence?

Why were John Adams's
last words so ironic?

ow that your brain has been inspired by alliteration and onomatopoeia, it's time to move on to some other literary devices. The following techniques will be used in all sorts of literature, from poems to novels, so they're great terms to know.

Dialogue is a conversation between two or more characters.

A **flashback** is a description of a past event that is inserted into a description of present action. For example, a person on a deathbed may flashback to the significant moments in his or her life.

An **allusion** is a reference to another literary work or a well-known example of history, music, or art. Stories and novels sometimes allude to other characters, events, or settings from other works of art and literature.

Irony is when words express something other than their actual meaning, often humorously. Irony often happens when there is a significant difference between what readers expect from a passage and what actually occurs in a passage. For example, it is ironic if a big weightlifter in a passage is named "Tiny" or if a skinny accountant is called "Big Tony."

The **mood** of a passage is the feeling and atmosphere that is created by everything that went into the passage, particularly the setting and imagery. It is the emotion that the passage is trying to make you feel.

The **tone** of a passage is the narrator's attitude toward the characters and events in the passage. When people talk, you can often tell by their tone of voice if they are angry, happy, upset, or whatever. The tone of a passage can tell you the same thing.

The tone is related to (and often confused with) the mood of a passage. The difference is that the tone comes from how the person telling the story feels about things in the story, whereas the mood comes from you, the reader, as the emotion that you feel as you read.

Alfred Nobel: A Noble Man

The nineteenth-century Swedish scientist and inventor Alfred Nobel is best known for the prize he created a fund for: the Nobel Prize. The Nobel Prize is given each year to the individual or organization who made the most significant contributions to humanity in a specific field, such as peace, literature, and medicine. But the man whose name is now synonymous with peace was also responsible for inventing dynamite.

In 1867, Nobel invented the explosive dynamite—the key element used in many bombs at that time. However, Nobel was interested in dynamite for nonmilitary purposes, such as tunneling through mountains for roads, and Nobel himself was a pacifist (meaning he did not believe in war). Instead, dynamite was used to create some of the most powerful weapons ever used in war at that time.

▶ What is ironic about Alfred Nobel's life?

_____

_____

Know It All Approach

Irony is a complex term. One way to think of it is a word or expression that means the opposite of what it usually means. Knowing that, what is ironic in the life of Alfred Nobel? Read the passage carefully, and look for the example where something means or acts to the contrary.

Alfred Nobel is associated with the Nobel Peace Prize. This prestigious award is given to the person or organization who is responsible for advancements in *peace.* However, Nobel is also associated with dynamite, the destructive explosive that he invented in 1867 and that we tend to associate with war. It is ironic that a promoter of peace contributed to a technology of war. You wouldn't expect that, would you?

The fact that Alfred Nobel invented dynamite, an explosive used in weapons, and set up an international peace prize is conflicting. The two concepts—war and peace—are opposite. That is something ironic about Alfred Nobel's life.

 Hip History

Thomas Jefferson Still Survives

1   Dark clouds gathered overhead on the miserable Massachusetts morning of July 4, 1826. John Adams, the second president of the United States, lay ill in his bed, halfway between life and death at ninety years of age. As old age crept into his blood, Adams knew his time on Earth was nearly complete.

2   I survived to witness the fiftieth birthday of my country, Adams gravely thought to himself. It was exactly fifty years since he had signed the Declaration of Independence. "I always thought I would outlive Jefferson," he muttered, referring to Thomas Jefferson, the third U.S. president.

3   Jefferson and Adams had been friends at the founding of the country. In fact, Jefferson and Adams had both signed the Constitution in Philadelphia in 1776. But shortly thereafter, the two men became bitter enemies. They both wanted to be president after George Washington left office. John Adams, a Federalist, disagreed on many political opinions with Thomas Jefferson, the leader of the rival Democratic-Republican Party.

4   John Adams was elected the second president of the United States by a narrow margin. Four years later, in 1800, Jefferson beat Adams in the following election. The two men remained enemies for many years. Eventually, Adams and Jefferson become friends again, writing letters to each other in their old age. And as Adams lay in bed, he closed his tired eyes and drifted back into the past.

5   "Benjamin Franklin is sick!" was the cry heard in Philadelphia fifty years before. Franklin would have been expected to write the Declaration, but he was too sick. "Someone needs to draft the document to free us from Great Britain!" The responsibility thus almost fell on forty-year-old Adams's shoulders as the representative of the New England colonies. Some of the delegates thought he was the best man for the job. But Adams knew better. Adams, along with many delegates, thought Thomas Jefferson was destined to draft the document. Sure, the thirty-three-year-old Virginian was shy and not a good speaker, but he was a brilliant writer.

6   Yet with each of John Adams's attempts to convince Thomas Jefferson to take up his pen, Jefferson flatly refused. The stubborn Adams would not accept that, however. In one last plea to the Virginian, he is said to have told Jefferson, "You write it! You are ten times the writer I am."

7   Jefferson agreed and spent the next three weeks drafting the words that were to become so familiar to generations of Americans. He wrote of self-evident truths. He wrote that all men are created equal. He wrote that it is the right of men to life, liberty, and the pursuit of happiness. He declared the colonies to be free and independent.

8   The Declaration had been a success. The thought brought Adams some comfort as he felt the life drain from his body on the cold bed. The country had been a success. His long life had been a success—even if he hadn't outlasted Jefferson, now eighty-three years old.

9   As he stumbled out of consciousness for the last time, Adams whispered his final words, "Thomas Jefferson still survives." Little did he know that several hours earlier Jefferson had died in his Virginia home. Because communication was so slow in the early 1800s, no one in Massachusetts knew this until much later.

Directions: Answer questions 1–8 based on the passage about John Adams and Thomas Jefferson.

1. Based on information in the article, the reader can conclude that the narrator's tone is

    A respectful.
    B overjoyed.
    C anxious.
    D angry.

2. Which of the following paragraphs in the passage contains an example of a flashback?

    A first and second
    B third and eighth
    C fifth and sixth
    D seventh and eighth

3. What clue helps the reader understand that Adams's flashbacks are about events in the past?

    _____

    _____

4. What fact concerning John Adams's death was ironic?

    A Adams died on the same day as Thomas Jefferson.
    B Adams died in his home in Massachusetts at age ninety.
    C Adams died on the fiftieth anniversary of the signing of the Declaration of Independence.
    D Adams's final words were "Thomas Jefferson still survives," hours after Jefferson had passed away.

5. Which line from the story contains alliteration?

    A   Dark clouds gathered overhead on the miserable Massachusetts morning of July 4, 1826.
    B   In fact, Jefferson and Adams had both signed the Constitution together in Philadelphia in 1776.
    C   John Adams was elected the second president of the United States by a narrow margin.
    D   Franklin was supposed to write the Declaration, but he was too sick.

6. How would you describe the mood of the passage?

    A   antagonistic
    B   informative
    C   cheerful
    D   complaining

7. Which phrase from the story alludes to the Declaration of Independence?

    A   the leader of the rival Democratic-Republican Party
    B   fell on forty-year-old Adams's shoulders
    C   life, liberty, and the pursuit of happiness
    D   Adams whispered his final words

8. Write a sentence from the story that is an example of dialogue between two characters.

    _____

    _____

Subject Review

Literary devices contribute to the feelings passages inspire. They can add depth to a story and make references to other works of literature. They are powerful writing tools. To refresh your memory, the literary devices from this chapter are listed below.

Dialogue is a conversation between two or more characters.

A **flashback** is a description of a past event that is inserted into a description of present action.

An **allusion** is a reference to another literary work or a well-known example of history, music, or art.

Irony is when words express something other than their actual meaning, often humorously. Irony often happens when there is a significant difference between what readers expect from a passage and what actually occurs in a passage.

The **mood** of a passage is the feeling and atmosphere that is created by everything that went into the passage, particularly the setting and imagery.

The **tone** of a passage is the narrator's attitude toward the characters and events in the passage.

And now, of course, here are the solutions to the questions at the start of the chapter.

What did the man who invented dynamite do to promote peace?

Alfred Nobel, a Swedish chemist, invented dynamite. Although his invention was used in bombs and other destructive means, Nobel wanted to ensure that his name would be remembered for more noble causes. He established the Nobel Prizes, given every year for several categories, the most notable being the Nobel Peace Prize.

Who convinced Thomas Jefferson to write the Declaration of Independence?

Originally, Benjamin Franklin was expected to write the Declaration of Independence. When he fell ill, John Adams was asked to write the document. But he convinced Thomas Jefferson to write it because he felt Jefferson would do an excellent job. He was right!

Why were John Adams's last words so ironic?

The last words of the second U.S. president John Adams were "Thomas Jefferson still survives." However, he was unaware that Jefferson had passed away several hours earlier. So Adams's last words were ironic because they were the opposite of the truth.

Outer Space Oddities

Mark Twain and Halley's Comet

Halley's comet orbits the Sun every seventy-six years. When it came near Earth in November 1835, the American writer Mark Twain was born. He spent his life as a writer and a humorist, penning many famous novels. When he was seventy-five years old, Twain said, "I came in with Halley's comet in 1835. It is coming again next year, and I expect to go out with it." Twain died on April 21, 1910—one day after the comet's closest approach to Earth in seventy-six years.

Below is an excerpt from one of Twain's most beloved books, *The Adventures of Huckleberry Finn.*

> "YOU don't know about me without you have read a book by the name of The Adventures of Tom Sawyer; but that ain't no matter. That book was made by Mr. Mark Twain, and he told the truth, mainly. There was things which he stretched, but mainly he told the truth. That is nothing. I never seen anybody but lied one time or another, without it was Aunt Polly, or the widow, or maybe Mary. Aunt Polly—Tom's Aunt Polly, she is—and Mary, and the Widow Douglas is all told about in that book, which is mostly a true book, with some stretchers, as I said before.
>
> Now the way that the book winds up is this: Tom and me found the money that the robbers hid in the cave, and it made us rich. We got six thousand dollars apiece—all gold. It was an awful sight of money when it was piled up. Well, Judge Thatcher he took it and put it out at interest, and it fetched us a dollar a day apiece all the year round—more than a body could tell what to do with. The Widow Douglas she took me for her son, and allowed she would sivilize me; but it was rough living in the house all the time, considering how dismal regular and decent the widow was in all her ways; and so when I couldn't stand it no longer I lit out. I got into my old rags and my sugar-hogshead again, and was free and satisfied. But Tom Sawyer he hunted me up and said he was going to start a band of robbers, and I might join if I would go back to the widow and be respectable. So I went back.

The widow she cried over me, and called me a poor lost lamb, and she called me a lot of other names, too, but she never meant no harm by it. She put me in them new clothes again, and I couldn't do nothing but sweat and sweat, and feel all cramped up. Well, then, the old thing commenced again. The widow rung a bell for supper, and you had to come to time. When you got to the table you couldn't go right to eating, but you had to wait for the widow to tuck down her head and grumble a little over the victuals, though there warn't really anything the matter with them,—that is, nothing only every-thing was cooked by itself. In a barrel of odds and ends it is differ-ent; things get mixed up, and the juice kind of swaps around, and the things go better . . . . . "

Directions: Answer questions 1–3 about Mark Twain and *The Adventures of Huckleberry Finn*.

1. Which phrase from the story contains an example of irony?

   A   but it was rough living in the house all the time
   B   he was going to start a band of robbers, and I might join if I would go back to the widow and be respectable
   C   and she called me a lot of other names, too, but she never meant no harm by it
   D   but you had to wait for the widow to tuck down her head and grumble a little over the victuals

2. How is Huckeberry Finn different from the widow who is taking care of him?

   _____

   _____

3. To what book does this introduction to *The Adventures of Huckleberry Finn* allude?

   _____

CHAPTER 11

Figurative Language

Why do moths like to fly directly into flaming candles?

Why do clouds float?

Can a cockroach write poetry?

By now you've reviewed everything from alliteration and allusions to flashbacks and free verse, and your *Know It All* brain is so huge, it's practically dripping out of your ears. But there are a few other literary techniques of which you should be aware. These are different ways of using figurative language.

Figurative language is a type of literary technique in which authors use words or phrases to represent something other than what they actually mean. Metaphor, simile, and personification are examples of figurative language. Each of these techniques makes a piece of writing richer and more original.

- A **simile** makes a comparison between two unlike things by using the words *like* or *as*. For example, Bill acted like a baby when his team lost the game. He threw a temper tantrum, cried uncontrollably, and stomped his feet angrily.

- A **metaphor** makes a comparison between two unlike things without using the words *like* or *as*. For example, the eagle was a jet plane soaring through the clouds.

- **Personification** describes an object, animal, or idea using human characteristics. For example, if ripples on an ocean caused the moon's reflection to move, you could say, "The moonlight danced upon the water." Dancing is a human characteristic, but you could describe the moon as doing it too. That's personification.

Remember: Figurative language doesn't provide facts. It describes things imaginatively. Therefore, be very careful not to read it literally. So when you read, "the eagle was a jet plane," don't think of a bird soaring in the sky with a set of jet engines attached to its wings. And when you read, "the moonlight danced," don't imagine the light doing a waltz in a ballroom. Those examples are just figures of speech—figurative language.

Metaphors and similes are very similar. They both compare two things. The difference is that simile uses the words *like* or *as*. It's a pretty important difference, so don't you forget it!

The Entertainment Center

For Janis

Janis Joplin was one of the greatest blues-rock singers of the 1960s. She was a songbird with a beautiful voice that was both soulful and haunting. Joplin became a superstar in the summer of 1967 when she performed in the Monterey Pop Festival in California. About 200,000 people attended the event and many became big fans. In the summer of 1969, she sang for nearly 500,000 people at the famous Woodstock Music and Art Festival in New York.

Joplin's biggest hits included "Piece of My Heart" and "Try (Just a Little Bit Harder)." The song "Me and Bobby McGee" reached number one on the charts in 1971. Unfortunately, Pearl, as Joplin was nicknamed, passed away in 1970. Joplin was inducted into the Rock and Roll Hall of Fame in 1995. Today, many people still consider her one of the most talented singers of the twentieth century.

▶ Which part of the passage contains a metaphor?

A   Janis Joplin was one of the greatest blues-rock singers.
B   She was a songbird with a beautiful voice.
C   About 200,000 people attended the event.
D   Pearl was inducted into the Rock and Roll Hall of Fame.

Know It All Approach

This question tests your knowledge of the type of figurative language called a **metaphor**. A metaphor is a way to compare two things without using the word *like* or *as*. Did you find any metaphors when you read the passage? If you didn't notice, that's okay. This is a multiple-choice question, so you can look at the answer choices for a metaphor.

Start with answer choice (A). It states that Joplin was a great singer. You could say this phrase compares her to a great singer, so maybe this choice is right. Hold on to it and look for a better option.

Answer choice (B) should scream out, "I'm a metaphor!" It says she was a bird. Did she fly into windows, peck at bird food, or make a mess on a new car? No, no, and no. She was not a real bird. It is a metaphor meaning she sang beautifully like a bird. This looks like the right answer choice, but check (C) and (D) to be sure.

Neither answer choice (C) nor (D) doesn't use any figurative language. Both choices simply state facts using straightforward sentences. You can eliminate them. Answer choice (B) is correct.

Mad Science

Have you ever wondered why clouds float? Because if clouds are made of water, and water is heavier than air, why in the world would clouds float? The truth is that the billions of tiny water particles in clouds are so tiny that gravity doesn't affect them very much. They act like dust particles, which can float in the air without being affected very much by gravity. Are clouds lonely? Well, William Wordsworth seems to think so.

Daffodils
by William Wordsworth

I wandered lonely as a cloud
That floats on high o'er vales and hills,
When all at once I saw a crowd,
A host, of golden daffodils,
Beside the lake, beneath the trees,   **5**
Fluttering and dancing in the breeze.

Continuous as the stars that shine
And twinkle on the milky way,
They stretched in never-ending line
Along the margin of a bay: **10**
Ten thousand saw I at a glance,
Tossing their heads in sprightly dance.

The waves beside them danced; but they
Out-did the sparkling waves in glee;
A poet could not but be gay,   **15**
In such jocund company;
I gazed—and gazed—but little thought
What wealth the show to me had brought;

For oft, when on my couch I lie
In vacant or in pensive mood,   **20**
They flash upon that inward eye
Which is the bliss of solitude;
And then my heart with pleasure fills,
And dances with the daffodils.

Directions: Answer questions 1–4 based on William Wordsworth's poem, "Daffodils."

1. Is the first line of the poem, "I wandered lonely as a cloud" an example of a simile or a metaphor? How do you know?

   _____

   _____

2. Which line from the poem gives an example of personification?

   A   line 5
   B   line 6
   C   line 10
   D   line 11

3. What is another line from the poem that gives an example of personification?

   A   line 13
   B   line 15
   C   line 17
   D   line 19

4. Write an example of figurative language from the second stanza of the poem. Tell what type of figurative language it is, and why.

   _____

   _____

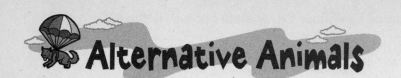

Alternative Animals

If you've ever spent time on a lighted porch or by a toasty campfire, you know moths love bright light. They swoop near flames and hang by light bulbs as if light bulbs are the place to be. Although scientists can't ask moths why, they have a theory: Moths developed a flight plan based on the light of the Moon. They can fly toward it, and that helps them keep direction. When moths see a brighter light—like a light bulb—they get confused and use the brighter light for navigation. Unlike the Moon, they can fly right into the torch and sizzle. Oops.

The Lesson of the Moth
by Archy the cockroach (Don Marquis)

i was talking to a moth
the other evening
he was trying to break into
an electric light bulb
and fry himself on the wires   **5**

why do you fellows
pull this stunt i asked him
because it is the conventional
thing for moths or why
if that had been an uncovered   **10**
candle instead of an electric
light bulb you would
now be a small unsightly cinder
have you no sense

plenty of it he answered   **15**
but at times we get tired
of using it
we get bored with the routine
and crave beauty
and excitement   **20**
fire is beautiful
and we know that if we get
too close it will kill us
but what does that matter
it is better to be happy   **25**
for a moment
and be burned up with beauty
than to live a long time
and be bored all the while

so we wad all our life up   30
into one little roll
and then we shoot the roll
that is what life is for
it is better to be a part of beauty
for one instant and then cease to   35
exist than to exist forever
and never be a part of beauty
our attitude toward life
is come easy go easy
we are like human beings   40
used to be before they became
too civilized to enjoy themselves

and before i could argue him
out of his philosophy
he went and immolated himself   45
on a patent cigar lighter
i do not agree with him
myself i would rather have
half the happiness and twice
the longevity   50

but at the same time i wish
there was something i wanted
as badly as he wanted to fry himself

Directions: Answer questions 5–6 based on Archy's poem.

5. What type of figurative language forms the basis for this poem?

   A   simile
   B   metaphor
   C   personification
   D   imagery

6. Write one example of how figurative language is used in this poem.

   _____

   _____

Subject Review

All right! Make sure your brain got all that information about similes, metaphors, and personification by reading the following review.

A **simile** makes a comparison between two unlike things by using either the word *like* or the word *as.*

A **metaphor** makes a comparison between two unlike things without using the words *like* or *as.*

Personification describes an object, animal, or idea using human characteristics.

By now you might be wondering what was up with that cockroach poet in the question on page 97. Well, below are the answers to that question and the others from the beginning of the chapter.

Why do moths like to fly directly into flaming candles?
Nobody is exactly sure because moths can't talk (even though Archy the cockroach can). Scientists theorize it's because moths think the light is the Moon, and they use the Moon as a navigational guide. Another theory is that moths fly up to escape danger, and they know that the Moon is up. So they fly up toward the light—even manmade light. They are not the smartest creatures.

Why do clouds float?
Even though clouds can actually be very, very heavy, they are made up of very light water particles. They are so light, in fact, that gravity does not have very much pull on them. Winds also help keep the water in clouds airborne.

Can a cockroach write poetry?
Yes! Okay, not really. The poet Don Marquis created an imaginary character named Archy, a cockroach. In Marquis's mind, the roach had to jump onto the letters of the typewriter to write his poems. (That's why it couldn't capitalize the letters in the poem.)

Know It All! Middle School Reading

CHAPTER 12
Point of View and Characterization

How old was Bobby Fischer when he won his first U.S. championship?

How far did the Apollo 13 astronauts have to travel after their oxygen tank exploded?

There are many different perspectives, or points of view, from which a story can be told. Sometimes it is told by a person who is actually in the story. Sometimes the passage is told from someone who is not involved but who seems to be watching from the outside.

The **narrator** is the person telling the story. You might have noticed that many of the passages in this book are told by narrators with different perspectives. Back in chapter 6, the passage about fireflies is told from a person who is also in the story. The girl walking with her brother Zenon participated in the action. But in chapter 5 the passage about Lazy Gene is told from someone outside the story. The difference between the two passages is the narrator's point of view.

The **point of view** is the perspective of the narrator. It shows how the narrator or author views the passage and the characters in the story. The point of view is called **first person** if the narrator is involved in the story. First-person narrators often use the words *I, me,* and *my.* The point of view is called **third person** if the narrator is not in the story. Third-person narrators can describe how other characters feel and think.

Characters are those who perform the actions in a passage.

The **author** is the person who wrote the passage. It doesn't matter whether the narrator is a person in the story or an outsider; the author remains the same. Only in an autobiography is the author and the narrator the same person.

The author creates **characterization** by including details about the personality and motivations of each character in a passage. Those details include what that character says and how that character behaves. Characterization tells you about the people in the stories.

Go back to the excerpt from the first chapter of Mark Twain's *The Adventures of Huckleberry Finn* on pages 95–96. Give it another read, and pay close attention to the narrator's point of view and the author's use of characterization. Here are (even more!) questions about this passage.

▶ Who is the author of the excerpt? _____

▶ Who is the narrator and what is his point of view? _____

▶ Write an example of how characterization is used and what it tells you about the character.

_____

_____

Know It All Approach

This series of questions tests your knowledge of the terms from the previous page. (Standardized tests will test this knowledge too.)

Even though the words seem to come from Huckleberry Finn's mouth, the author is the person who wrote them. That means Mark Twain is the author. Twain uses informal language to give the narrator his voice. So while Twain is the writer, he assigns the job of the narrator to Huck Finn.

The story is told from the point of view of Huck. Huck is the narrator of the passage.

There are many different examples of characterization in this excerpt. Any clue that tells you about a character in the story is characterization. For example, the Widow Douglas who took Huck "for her son" tries to dress him in new clothes. Huck says that he feels cramped in them. His "old rags" made him feel "free and satisfied." Huck Finn also doesn't understand why he couldn't eat when he got to the table. These should help characterize Finn as a wild, loose, and free-spirited character and the widow as a proper, "regular" caretaker.

These are good answers to these questions.

Mark Twain is the author of the passage.

Huck Finn is the narrator of the passage. His point of view is the first person.

The Widow Douglas who took Huck "for her son" tries to dress him in new clothes. Huck says that he feels cramped in them. His "old rags" made him feel "free and satisfied."

Huck Finn also doesn't understand why he couldn't eat when he got to the table. These help characterize Finn as a wild, loose, and free-spirited character and the widow as a proper, "regular" caretaker.

Searching to Become Bobby Fischer

I stared at the chessboard in disbelief. I was going to lose a tournament game to a player who was two years younger than I was. My opponent, Max, could put my king in mate in only three moves. I only hoped that he didn't see the opportunity. No such luck. He moved his bishop into position, setting up the end of the game.

I looked sadly over at my mom who was standing at the side of the room. She knew the game was over but flashed a smile and a thumbs-up sign anyway. Back at the chessboard, I made a few last meaningless moves to make the game official and walked away from the board as fast as I could—straight to my mom.

"Not everybody can be Bobby Fischer, Greg," my mom said. She knew how I always wanted to be like Bobby Fischer, the mysterious, eccentric, and brilliant chess champion. Fischer was the U.S. Chess Champion when he was only fourteen years old. I had turned thirteen the week before, and I wasn't anywhere close to winning a championship—an eleven-year-old just beat me!

I realized I was not going to be an International Grandmaster by the time I turned fifteen like Bobby Fischer, either. Tears started to well up in my eyes, and I started feeling nauseous. My mom didn't say a word, but she hugged me a little harder. She was really good at making me feel better, even if she didn't say anything.

As we were getting ready to leave the competition room, I saw Max approaching me. What could *he* want? I tried to wipe my eyes so it wouldn't look like I was so upset.

"You played a great game," Max said as he caught up to me. "I especially liked the way you used your knights to attack. If you could have advanced your rooks, I think you would have had me." He extended his hand toward me.

For a second, I didn't know how to react. I looked up at my mom, and she just smiled. Then I turned to Max and proudly shook his hand.

"Thanks a lot, Max. It was a great game," I said. Already the sick feeling in my stomach was gone. "Maybe some day you can be the next Bobby Fischer!"

Directions: Answer questions 1–3 based on the passage *Searching to Become Bobby Fischer.*

1. Who is the narrator of this short story?

   A   Bobby Fischer

   B   Max

   C   Greg

   D   Greg's mom

2. How does the narrator in the short story feel about Bobby Fischer? Explain how you know this.

   _____

   _____

3. Based on the information in the passage, what is the best adjective for describing Max?

   A   rude

   B   gracious

   C   mysterious

   D   cruel

The Perspective from Space

"Houston, we've had a problem," said Jim Lovell, commander of the *Apollo 13* mission. His message beamed at light speed back to mission control on Earth, about 200,000 miles away. Lovell was on his fourth trip to space (more trips than anyone else had taken at that time), but he had never had this problem before.

"And we had a pretty large bang," added Fred Haise, the lunar module pilot for *Apollo 13*. Haise was the pilot who was going to land on the Moon when *Apollo* got closer.

Nearly fifty-six hours into the third mission to the Moon, one of *Apollo 13*'s oxygen tanks had overheated and blown up, damaging the other oxygen tank. The explosion also cut power to two of three fuel cells.

Lovell knew what that meant; NASA did not allow Moon landings with only one fuel cell, so the Moon landing was clearly off. Neither Lovell, Haise, nor Jack Swigert, the third crewmember of *Apollo 13*, had ever been to the Moon before. Lovell was disappointed; he had always wanted to go to the Moon. He sighed out loud, resigned to the fact that it simply wasn't going to happen, and looked out the window; the Moon was so close, he felt like he could almost touch it.

There wasn't much time to be disappointed, however. Precious oxygen was rapidly escaping from *Apollo 13* into space, and the crew was very, very far from home. Just then, Lovell thought of his wife, Marilyn, and forgot about his frustration completely.

We've got to get to work, Lovell thought to himself. Lovell knew that there was a lot to do to survive the rest of the trip. The explosions had destroyed essential water and propellant supplies. *It is going to take a whole lot of cleverness and creativity to get home safely,* thought Lovell. *It is time to focus.*

Directions: Answer questions 4–6 based on the passage from page 110.

4. Who was the narrator of this story? Explain how you know this.

   _____

   _____

5. Describe the characteristics of Jim Lovell using details from the passage.

   _____

   _____

   _____

6. How do you think Jim Lovell felt at the end of this passage?

   A   saddened
   B   relieved
   C   frustrated
   D   determined

Subject Review

After finishing this chapter, you should be clear on point of view and the differences among the author, the narrator, and the characters in a story. In case you need to refresh your memory, here are the important terms to know.

Characters perform the actions in a passage.

The **narrator** is the one telling the passage.

The **author** is the person who wrote the passage.

The **point of view** is the perspective of the narrator or author. It shows how the narrator or author views the passage and the characters in the passage.

Characterization is created by the details about the personality and motivations of a character in a passage, including what that character says and how that character behaves.

Now, the answers you've been waiting for.

How old was Bobby Fischer when he won his first U.S. championship?

Bobby Fischer was only fourteen years old when he won his first U.S. championship. He was also the U.S. champion several more times as a teenager! In fact, he entered the U.S. championship eight times in his life—and he won every time!

How far did the Apollo 13 astronauts have to travel after their oxygen tank exploded?

The astronauts in *Apollo 13* were a mind-boggling 200,000 miles from Earth when their oxygen tank exploded. To get home, they needed to circle the Moon before turning back. That made the total distance they traveled with a minimum of water and power about 300,000 miles. That would be like traveling from California to New York—100 times!

CHAPTER 13
Conflict, Plot, Setting, and Sequence

What contest resulted in the creation of one of the greatest books in the nineteenth century?

How old was Mary Wollstonecraft Shelley when she wrote Frankenstein?

Why did the monster in the book Frankenstein vow to hate mankind?

As your *Know It All* brain learned in previous chapters, all kinds of people are involved in a story—there are the people who do the action and the people behind the scenes who just tell you what is going on.

But what about the other stuff that happens in a story? What about all the action, the surroundings, and the whole idea of a story? That's what this chapter is about.

Every good story involves at least some sort of action. It doesn't have to be as dramatic as a passionate fencing duel or a bloody battle; it may even involve action that takes place inside a character's head. Whatever the case, the action usually arises from conflict. **Conflict** is the reason the action in the passage takes place. It is the struggle between the opposing forces in a passage. For example, in the passage about Huck Finn and the widow on pages 95–96, the two characters have a conflict because they like to live in different ways.

The conflict in a story is only one part of what's going on. You also have the **setting** of the story—the time and place in which a passage occurs. The setting could be on a river raft in the 1800s (like in *The Adventures of Huckleberry Finn*). It could also be a chess tournament that takes place in the modern day. (Sound familiar?) The details of the scenery add to the setting to make a richer context for a story.

The **sequence** in a story is the order of the events in a passage. The sequence is often chronological, meaning it starts from the beginning and goes forward in time. But sometimes flashbacks take the reader to times in the past.

All of these parts of a story help to make up its plot. The **plot** is the series of events that the action of the narrative is centered around. Basically, the plot is what happens in a passage. For example, here is the plot of *The Adventures of Huckleberry Finn*,

> *After being kidnapped by his abusive father, Huck Finn fakes his death to escape. Together with Jim, a runaway slave, Huck travels down the Mississippi River on a raft in search for freedom. While Huck and Jim are on their terrific journey, they encounter interesting people and experience wild adventures. For example, they meet the Grangerfords and the Shepheredsons and the Duke and Dauphin. Huck learns about society and slavery. Jim is sold back into slavery, and Huck works to free him from it.*

Art-rageous

Just Like Frank N. Stein

Eighteen-year-old Mary Wollstonecraft Godwin was on her summer vacation in Switzerland with a few friends. Cold and steady rain kept the vacationers indoors, and they read scary ghost stories to each other to stay entertained through the gloomy weather. Then someone suggested that they should write their *own* creepy ghost stories!

The friends began to write their stories, but Godwin could not think of a good plot. She lay awake trying to top her friends' terrifying tales. Then suddenly a deep, dark, nightmarish vision entered her head, and the story of Frankenstein was born within her imagination. Godwin put her story to the written page, and by the next summer her novel was complete. *Frankenstein* was published on January 1, 1818, under Godwin's married name: Mary Wollstonecraft Shelley.

The following excerpt is from Mary Shelley's novel, *Frankenstein.*

I spent the following day roaming through the valley. I stood beside the sources of the Arveiron, which take their rise in a glacier, that with slow pace is advancing down from the summit of the hills to barricade the valley. The abrupt sides of vast mountains were before me; the icy wall of the glacier overhung me; a few shattered pines were scattered around; and the solemn silence of this glorious presence-chamber of imperial nature was broken only by the brawling waves or the fall of some vast fragment, the thunder sound of the avalanche or the cracking, reverberated along the mountains, of the accumulated ice

▶ What is the setting of this excerpt?

_____

_____

Know It All Approach

This open-response question asks you to describe the setting. Look for details that tell you where the story is taking place.

Even though it isn't clear what time period this excerpt is from, you know that the setting is in nature. There is no description of a city. This part of the story takes place in the wild. Here is a possible response to the question based on the information in the excerpt.

The narrator is beside a slow river fed from a nearby glacier, in a valley of vast

mountains. The area was lifeless and eerily quiet, with the booming sound of the

glacier cracking disrupting the silence.

The following is another excerpt from Mary Shelley's *Frankenstein*. This part of the story is told from the point of view of the monster as he talked to his creator, Victor Frankenstein.

"My travels were long and the sufferings I endured intense. It was late in autumn when I quitted the district where I had so long resided. I traveled only at night, fearful of encountering the visage of a human being. Nature decayed around me, and the sun became heatless; rain and snow poured around me; mighty rivers were frozen; the surface of the earth was hard and chill, and bare, and I found no shelter. Oh, earth! How often did I imprecate curses on the cause of my being! The mildness of my nature had fled, and all within me was turned to gall and bitterness. The nearer I approached to your habitation, the more deeply did I feel the spirit of revenge enkindled in my heart. Snow fell, and the waters were hardened, but I rested not. A few incidents now and then directed me, and I possessed a map of the country; but I often wandered wide from my path. The agony of my feelings allowed me no respite; no incident occurred from which my rage and misery could not extract its food; but a circumstance that happened when I arrived on the confines of Switzerland, when the sun had recovered its warmth and the earth again began to look green, confirmed in an especial manner the bitterness and horror of my feelings.

"I generally rested during the day and travelled only when I was secured by night from the view of man. One morning, however, finding that my path lay through a deep wood, I ventured to continue my journey after the sun had risen; the day, which was one of the first of spring, cheered even me by the loveliness of its sunshine and the balminess of the air. I felt emotions of gentleness and pleasure, that had long appeared dead, revive within me. Half surprised by the novelty of these sensations, I allowed myself to be borne away by them, and forgetting my solitude and deformity, dared to be happy. Soft tears again bedewed my cheeks, and I even raised my humid eyes with thankfulness towards the blessed sun, which bestowed such joy upon me.

"I continued to wind among the paths of the wood, until I came to its boundary, which was skirted by a deep and rapid river, into which many of the trees bent their branches, now budding with the fresh spring. Here I paused, not exactly knowing what path to pursue, when I heard the sound of voices, that induced me to conceal myself under the shade of a cypress. I was scarcely hid when a young girl came running towards the spot where I was concealed, laughing, as if she ran from someone in sport. She continued her course along the precipitous sides of the river, when suddenly her foot slipped, and she fell into the rapid stream. I rushed from my hiding-place and with extreme labour, from the force of the current, saved her and dragged her to shore.

"She was senseless, and I endeavored by every means in my power to restore animation, when I was suddenly interrupted by the approach of a rustic, who was probably the person from whom she had playfully fled. On seeing me, he darted towards me, and tearing the girl from my arms, hastened towards the deeper parts of the wood. I followed speedily, I hardly knew why; but when the man saw me draw near, he aimed a gun, which he carried, at my body and fired. I sank to the ground, and my injurer, with increased swiftness, escaped into the wood.

"This was then the reward of my benevolence! I had saved a human being from destruction, and as a recompense I now writhed under the miserable pain of a wound which shattered the flesh and bone. The feelings of kindness and gentleness which I had entertained but a few moments before gave place to hellish rage and gnashing of teeth. Inflamed by pain, I vowed eternal hatred and vengeance to all mankind. But the agony of my wound overcame me; my pulses paused, and I fainted."

If you haven't read *Frankenstein*, go out and get it today! It's a remarkable book full of conflict, a unique sequence of events, and a horrifying nineteenth-century setting that was inspired by Shelley's stay in Switzerland. Shelley also included numerous allusions to other great books, such as *Paradise Lost*.

Directions: Answer questions 1–6 based on the excerpt from *Frankenstein.*

1. Which phrase from this excerpt of *Frankenstein* best illustrates the setting?

   A *which was skirted by a deep and rapid river, into which many of the trees bent their branches, now budding with the fresh spring*

   B *I was scarcely hid when a young girl came running towards the spot where I was concealed*

   C *I had saved a human being from destruction, and as a recompense I now writhed under the miserable pain of a wound*

   D *She was senseless, and I endeavoured by every means in my power to restore animation*

2. Which of the following occurred last in the excerpt?

   A The girl slipped and fell into the rapid stream.
   B The monster hid in the shade of a cypress tree.
   C The monster vowed hatred and vengeance to mankind.
   D The man fired his gun and hit the monster with a bullet.

3. Describe how the conflict between the monster and the drowning girl's friend changed the monster's character.

   _____

   _____

   _____

   _____

4. What is the sequence of events in this excerpt?

   A   The monster speaks of the future of his own existence.
   B   Victor Frankenstein has a flashback to when he built the monster.
   C   The monster tells of his past encounters with humans in a conversation.
   D   The monster goes back in time to an earlier meeting with Victor Frankenstein.

5. Which of the following lines from the story does **not** show that the monster has a difficult time with humanity?

   A   *On seeing me, he darted towards me, and tearing the girl from my arms, hastened towards the deeper parts of the wood.*
   B   *I generally rested during the day and traveled only when I was secured by night from the view of man.*
   C   *I had saved a human being from destruction, and as a recompense I now writhed under the miserable pain of a wound which shattered the flesh and bone.*
   D   *She continued her course along the precipitous sides of the river, when suddenly her foot slipped, and she fell into the rapid stream.*

6. What is the plot of this small excerpt from the book *Frankenstein*?

   _____

   _____

   _____

Subject Review

Scared yet? Mary Shelley's *Frankenstein* is still a popular book nearly 200 years after she wrote it. That's because the story is not only scary and very well written but it also has an important message about humanity. Ever hear the expression, "Don't judge a book by its cover?" Frankenstein's monster was actually an intelligent, caring, and sensitive being. He just looked hideously ugly. As a result, he was treated poorly and lashed out at people. Let that be a lesson: Treat people nicely, or they could turn into a "monster"!

Okay, now it's time to review the terms from this chapter. Do you remember them? If so, great! If not, that's okay. Here they are again.

A **conflict** is the reason the action in the passage takes place, the struggle between the opposing forces in a passage.

The **plot** is the series of events that the action of the narrative is centered on, what happens in a passage.

The **sequence** is the order of events in a passage.

The **setting** is the time and place in which a passage takes place.

And now, here are the answers to the questions from page 113.

What contest resulted in the creation of one of the greatest books in the nineteenth century?
Mary Wollstonecraft Godwin was involved in a scary-story contest. Her friend, Lord Byron, challenged her and her friends to write the scariest story possible. While most of her friends never finished their stories, Mary's story became one of the greatest pieces of literature from the 1800s!

How old was Mary Wollstonecraft Shelley when she wrote Frankenstein?
Mary Wollstonecraft Godwin was only eighteen years old when she started to write the book, *Frankenstein*. By the time she finished the book (the following year), she had married Percy Shelley, taking on his name. So Mary Wollstonecraft Godwin started writing the book at eighteen, but Mary Wollstonecraft Shelley finished it when she was nineteen!

Why did the monster in the book Frankenstein vow to hate mankind?
The creature that Victor Frankenstein created must have been one of the most misunderstood monsters of all time. The monster did not originally want to hurt people. However, because he was so ugly, people treated him unkindly. One person even shot him for no reason! As a result, he vowed to hate mankind forever!

Bizarre Human Feats

King of the Cobras

Mohamed Noor Abdullah sauntered along the hot city streets of the tropical island of Penang, in northern Malaysia. He strutted confidently and wore a smug grin on his face. The fifty-one-year-old former zookeeper was on his way to the major shopping center in the area where he was going to break a world record. And he was going to be famous.

Several months earlier, Abdullah's son-in-law, Othman Ayeb, had earned worldwide fame by breaking a world record. Ayeb, a professional snake tamer, had spent twenty-seven days living in a cage with hundreds of poisonous serpents. Among those creatures were deadly cobras and other snakes.

Abdullah appreciated the feat, but he thought he could do even better. He stepped off the street and into the serpent-filled tank where he would spend at least the next twenty-eight days of his life. Without a hint of fear in his heart, Abdullah was as fearless as a lion.

Two hundred and fifty poisonous snakes were led into the small glass room where Abdullah was going to make his home. Abdullah got used to his new surroundings, even though many snakes found his bed to be the most comfortable place in the room. Their favorite spot was curled up under his mattress!

Abdullah's confidence was shaken early when the king cobras became agitated. The territorial cobras didn't like having to share the small space with so many other snakes. They lashed out violently, often killing other snakes in the tank. As new snakes were brought into the room, the angry cobras would kill other ones.

For a few days, it looked like Abdullah might have to cancel his record attempt. Eventually, however, he was able to take control. Abdullah was a bull, and he stubbornly showed the snakes that he was the boss. When the deadly serpents acted up, Abdullah would slap them on the head. At one point, Abdullah found that the snakes had elected a leader who prevented other snakes from attacking him.

After thirty-five days, Mohamed Noor Abdullah walked out of the snake tank without any serious bites—and with a brand new world record: most days spent in a room with 250 poisonous snakes!

Directions: Answer questions 1–5 based on the passage about Mohamed Noor Abdullah and the cobras.

1. Which sentence from the story shows an example of a simile?

   A   At one point, Abdullah found that the snakes had elected a leader who prevented other snakes from attacking him.

   B   Without a hint of fear in his heart, Abdullah was as fearless as a lion.

   C   Abdullah was a bull, and he stubbornly showed the snakes that he was the boss.

   D   When the deadly serpents acted up, Abdullah would slap them on the head.

2. Which statement is true about the setting of this passage?

   A   It takes place in nineteenth-century India.

   B   It takes place on a hot day in July.

   C   It takes place in a shopping center in Malaysia.

   D   It takes place in a snake farm in the country.

3. Which of these includes a metaphor?

   A   Without a hint of fear in his heart, Mohamed was as fearless as a lion.

   B   Their favorite spot was curled up under his mattress!

   C   He strutted confidently and wore a smug grin on his face.

   D   Mohamed was a bull, and he stubbornly showed the snakes that he was the boss.

4. From what point of view is this story being told?

   _____

   _____

5. Write an example from the story that shows personification.

   _____

   _____

CHAPTER 14
Cause and Effect

How big was the meteor
that scientists think
may have killed off
the dinosaurs?

What animal likes to
slime other animals
to death?

Is it possible to play a
musical instrument by
waving your hands in
thin air?

When you know about cause and effect, that means you know about how people and events are connected, which means that your big *Know It All* brain understands how things work. Plus, most standardized tests have many cause-and-effect questions, and if you know how to do them, the effect will be that you'll get higher scores!

The **cause** is the reason that an event occurs. It can be the reason for an action or for someone doing something. The **effect** is the result of an event. It is what happens because of an action or something that someone does.

In science class, the *cause* of a lava flow on a model volcano is mixing baking soda with vinegar. The *effect* is that you will see lots of tiny bubbles, and the lava will flow from the top of the volcano.

If you're bothering your science teacher and you throw a paper airplane at her, the paper airplane is the *cause* of your trouble. The *effect* of your mischief is that you might get detention, or your teacher may force you to write a paper on the flight aerodynamics of paper airplanes. (Please don't throw paper airplanes in school!)

If your dog ate your homework thinking it was food, that is a *cause.* If that is the reason why you couldn't hand in your homework, then the *effect* of your hungry dog's snack is that you can't hand in your homework.

A single cause doesn't have to result in only a single effect. Many times, one cause can create many effects, much like dropping a pebble in water creates a series of ripples. In fact, almost every event can be attributed to cause-and-effect in some way, and the connections are sometimes fairly complicated. The Pilgrims came to America to find religious freedom. The *cause* was that the Pilgrims were being mistreated in England. One *effect* was that they landed on Plymouth Rock in 1620. Other effects were that a new nation was begun, the Revolutionary War happened, and so on and so forth.

When you see the word *cause* in a passage, whether in a noun or verb form, underline it! This probably indicates a cause-and-effect relationship.

 **Mad Science**

Wha' Happened?

Scientists aren't exactly sure what caused dinosaurs to become extinct about sixty-five million years ago. That's because none of the scientists were around then to see what happened! But scientists used some detective work to find clues and come up with a theory. Most scientists now think that a giant meteor, measuring about six miles long and weighing about a quadrillion metric tons, slammed into Earth at hundreds of thousands of miles per hour.

When the mammoth meteor struck Earth, it caused a gigantic explosion. Large chunks of Earth and space rock were driven into the atmosphere, where they remained for a long time. The skies around Earth grew dark with the tons of dust in the air, and sunlight could not reach the planet's surface. As a result, many kinds of plants died out because they needed sunlight for food. Without those plants, the plant-eating dinosaurs died, and without them, the meat-eating dinosaurs died too. Whole species of dinosaurs died off, causing mass extinction.

▶ According to the passage, what were two effects of such a large meteor hitting Earth?

_____

_____

Know It All Approach

Read the passage and question carefully. This question asks you to write two effects of a large meteor hitting Earth. You may already know about the meteor theory and how it may have affected the dinosaurs, but don't use that knowledge! Only use details from the passage to answer a test question. A reading test will never expect you to have outside knowledge about a topic.

The cause is a giant meteor hitting Earth. Your job is to find two effects, or results, of that cause. Read the passage again if you don't remember. Look for the cause-and-effect relationship, and then plan your answer with the information. Don't forget that you need to write *two* effects.

The second paragraph of the short passage tells about the effects of the giant meteor hitting Earth. It caused an explosion. It caused the skies to grow dark. It caused the sunlight to be blocked. And it also caused many plants and animals to die, including the dinosaurs. Write two of these effects neatly and clearly using complete sentences, and you'll get full credit.

Alternative Animals

Wacky Defenses

Animals have to be careful not to get eaten. Some, such as rhinoceroses or elephants, have horns or tusks to protect themselves. Others, such as turtles or bees, have shells or stingers. Some animals go even further than that and really get wild to protect themselves. There are animals that spit poison, play dead, or spray and slime their way to safety. One animal, the swallowtail butterfly caterpillar, even looks like yucky bird poop to avoid being eaten!

You may have seen a skunk. These black-and-white creatures are often found in suburban areas and can be a real nuisance. If they feel threatened, some skunks will stomp their feet and lift their back legs up as a warning. If that doesn't work, the skunk will spray a stench that smells so putrid that it has caused people to throw up! If a skunk sprays you, you will probably smell terrible for days!

Hopefully you've never run into a creature that spits poison. If a spitting cobra is confronted with danger, it may spit venom in an eight-foot spray. It aims at the eyes of its attacker and can cause blindness and extreme pain. The green lynx spider also spits venom, but only as far as eight inches. And a fulmar chick defends itself with vomit, shooting a stream of yellow stomach oil up to five feet away—gross! Mountain climbers that approach a fulmar's nest may be in for an unpleasant surprise.

The expression, "playing possum," comes from the opossum. If the animal determines its life is in danger, it will roll on its side and act dead. Other animals do this too, including American hognose snakes and some kinds of doves. Many predators will not eat dead animals, so rolling over to play dead can be a lifesaver!

The hagfish lives near the bottom of the ocean, feeding on dead fish that sink down through the water. If a hagfish gets attacked, slime oozes from the pores in its body and forms a protective gel around the fish. Not only does the slime prevent attacks but it can also kill. Moray eels, for example, may suffocate in the slimy substance that the hagfish creates. Who knew that slime could be so deadly?

Directions: Answer questions 1–3 based on the passage from page 126.

1. What is the effect of the opossum playing dead?

   A   Predators run away scared.
   B   Predators smell terrible for days!
   C   Some predators won't eat the opossum.
   D   It suffocates the predators and kills them.

2. What would be the effect of causing a spitting cobra to feel threatened?

   _____

   _____

3. What could cause a hagfish to slime another animal to death?

   _____

   _____

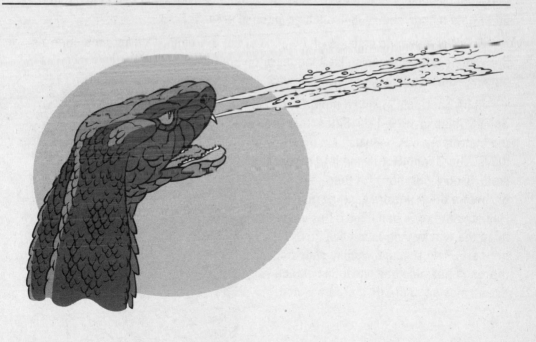

The Theremin

Did you know there is a musical instrument that you can play without touching it? You don't even have to blow into it, either. This magical instrument is called a theremin, and it creates a spooky, mysterious, and haunting noise.

The theremin is an electronic instrument that looks like a giant box. Sound waves are created inside the box. The sound waves cannot be picked up by the human ear unless a person interacts with the air around the instrument. There is a vertical antenna that sticks up at the back of the box. If you move your hand near that antenna, you break the sound field around it, which creates an electronic noise.

As you move your hand toward or away from the vertical antenna, you can also change the pitch of the instrument. That means you can change the notes by waving your hand in the air! As your hand approaches the vertical antenna, the theremin will emit a low-pitched noise. As you move your hand even closer, the pitch gets higher, sounding like a high-pitched screech.

There is a second antenna on the side of the theremin. This antenna controls the volume, and you can make it louder or quieter by moving your hand closer or farther away.

Leon Theremin invented the theremin in the Soviet Union in 1919–1920. Since its invention, the instrument has been used in a variety of ways. The Beach Boys used it to record the song "Good Vibrations," a theremin orchestra once performed at Carnegie Hall, and the rock band Phish has even used the wacky instrument live in concerts. The strange, wobbly sounding theremin has also been used in science fiction movies to create a creepy mood.

Directions: Answer questions 4–7 based on the passage about the theremin.

4. What causes the theremin to create high-pitched noises?

   A keeping your hand away from the antenna
   B waving your hand around the antenna
   C moving your hand close to the antenna
   D pulling on the second antenna on the side of the theremin

5. What effect does the sound of a theremin have on science fiction movies?

   A It creates a spooky mood for the movie.
   B It helps to characterize the people in the film.
   C It illustrates the plot of the movie.
   D It creates conflict in the action of the film.

6. If you break the sound field that surrounds the theremin with your hands, what will happen?

   A The instrument will break.
   B The instrument will make noise.
   C The pitch of the sound will change.
   D Your hands will be in a lot of pain.

7. Write one effect that Loon Theremin's invention has had on popular culture.

   _____

   _____

Subject Review

You've now seen how one event can cause another event to occur. The initial event is the **cause,** and the resulting event is the **effect.** Get used to seeing those words. You'll be seeing them for as long as you're in school—and for the rest of your life too. Life is made up of connected causes and effects and people who like to talk about them!

And now, just what you've been waiting for, the answers to the questions from page 123.

How big was the meteor that scientists think may have killed off the dinosaurs?

Scientists aren't even positive that a meteor was the cause of the dinosaurs going extinct. It is the most common theory, though. They think that the meteor must have been at least five miles across to cause such global damage—and probably even bigger. Thankfully, astronomers are always on the lookout for giant meteors heading our way!

What animal likes to slime other animals to death?

The strange hagfish can slime another animal to death. It secretes slime from the many glands all over its body. When the slime touches the saltwater from the ocean, it creates a gooey, thick mess. Some fish have choked to death in the slime.

Is it possible to play a musical instrument by waving your hands in the air?

You can play the theremin! You move your hands to control the volume and pitch, but you don't actually touch the instrument. Instead, your hands cause disturbances in a sound field, which affects the sound that the instrument makes. You can look at the picture on page 128 to see how it is played.

CHAPTER 15

Using Graphic Organizers

What contest features pumpkins catapulted thousands of feet in the air?

How far can an air cannon launch a pumpkin?

About how many hours of television does the average five-year-old watch per week?

A reading selection will often contain all kinds of bits of information. Each passage on a test may contain more than 1,000 words. Sometimes it helps to show what the passage tells you in a visual way. The best way to do that is with a graphic organizer.

Graphic organizers are visual representations of information. They can help you organize details. Graphic organizers may be in the form of tables, charts, diagrams, or graphs. You might even see questions on a test that will ask you to fill in a graphic organizer. It will help your *Know It All* brain to practice using as many graphic organizers as possible.

There are many kinds of graphic organizers. Some of them show the differences and similarities between two things—much like compare-and-contrast questions. A Venn diagram is a common graphic organizer that shows similarities and differences. Other graphic organizers illustrate the sequence of a story, such as the major events in a plot or the development of history. A graphic organizer can also break down the main ideas and supporting details from a passage into an understandable diagram. There are many, many valuable uses for a graphic organizer—and you have to admit, sometimes it's easier to sort out something with pictures than with words.

One type of graphic organizer you may be familiar with is the family tree. You would probably have a hard time if you had to show the generations of your family only using words. The task becomes much easier using a graphic organizer.

Go back to page 125 and reread the passage about the meteor theory. Pay special attention to the sequence of events, and then answer the following graphic organizer question.

▶ According to the meteor theory, the following four events occurred about sixty-five million years ago:

1   dinosaurs died off   3   many plants died
2   the skies became dark   4   an explosion occurred

Know It All Approach

Correctly order the events in the graphic organizer below. You should write the letter of each event in the proper box.

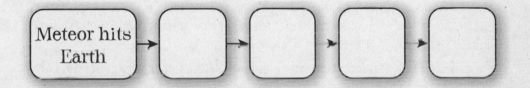

This question uses a graphic organizer to help tell the sequence of events from the passage about the meteor theory. You have to put the events in order based on when they happened. If you do it correctly, it will help you see the chain of events that may have occurred when the giant meteor crashed into Earth sixty-five million years ago.

Go back to the passage to review the events again. The passage says, "when the mammoth meteor struck Earth, it caused a gigantic explosion." So you know already that the event listed as (4) should be first in the series to follow "meteor hits Earth." Write (4) in the first empty box.

The passage then lists the effects of the meteor's explosion. It caused dust to fly into the air, causing blockage of the Sun. (2) is therefore the next step. The lack of sunlight killed off the plants, so (3) should follow in the third empty box. Finally, the dinosaurs died off as a result of having no plants (or plant-eating dinosaurs) to eat. The graphic organizer should look like the following:

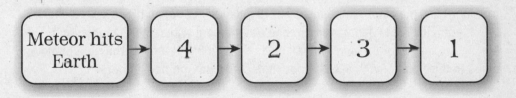

Extreme Sports

Punkin Chunkin Time

Is it a big, round bird? Is it a bright, orange plane? No, it's a flying pumpkin soaring thousands of feet in the air. You can you see this happen at the annual Punkin Chunkin event, a contest to see who can launch a pumpkin the farthest distance using catapults, springs, slingshots, pulleys, air cannons—anything but explosives—to propel the pumpkins as far as possible. The pumpkins must weigh between eight and ten pounds.

The peculiar contest began in Delaware in 1986 when a few friends challenged each other to build a pumpkin-tossing machine. Using springs connected to a car frame, the first winner of the Punkin Chunkin tossed a pumpkin 128 feet. By 2002, about 30,000 people were coming to witness pumpkins literally flying thousands of feet through the air.

There are many categories in which the contestants may now compete. For example, there is a youth division for competitors between the ages of eleven and seventeen. In this age group, the winner of the 2002 Punkin Chunkin was the team called Little Feats, which tossed a pumpkin 809 feet! In second place was Subjugator, with a distance of 427 feet. Pumpkin Beyond finished in third place, with a distance of 379 feet.

The giant catapults in the competition belong in their own category. For the 2002 competition, the catapult named Hypertension won its category by launching an eight-pound pumpkin 1,728 feet. Acme Catapult fell just short, with a total distance of 1,710 feet. In third place was a catapult called Feats Don't Fail Me Now, with a measured toss of 1,138 feet.

The biggest, baddest, most powerful machines in the whole Punkin Chunkin contest are the air cannons. These gigantic pieces of equipment use compressed air to shoot their pumpkins faster than 500 miles per hour! The 1999 Punkin Chunkin winner in the air cannon category, Big 10, has a lengthy barrel that measures 100 feet long! For the 2002 competition, Big 10 finished in second place with a shot of 3,817 feet. The 2002 winner was Second Amendment with a 3,882-foot launch. That's almost the length of thirteen football fields—about 3/4 of a mile! Universal Soldier came in third place, with a 3,632-foot shot. That's not too bad, either!

Directions: Use the information from page 134 to complete the graphic organizer below. Some of the details have already been filled in.

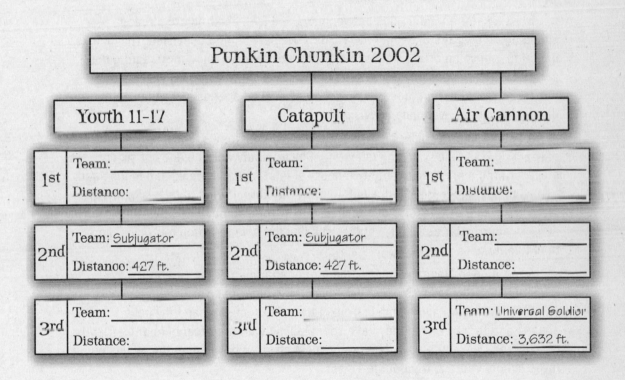

Punkin Chunkin 2002

Youth 11-17

1st Team: _____
Distance: _____

2nd Team: Subjugator
Distance: 427 ft.

3rd Team: _____
Distance: _____

Catapult

1st Team: _____
Distance: _____

2nd Team: Subjugator
Distance: 427 ft.

3rd Team: _____
Distance: _____

Air Cannon

1st Team: _____
Distance: _____

2nd Team: _____
Distance: _____

3rd Team: Universal Soldier
Distance: 3,632 ft.

The Entertainment Center

Frying Our Eyes Out

How often have you or someone in your family walked through the front door after a long day and headed right to the television set? Not long ago, there were no televisions at all, and now people spend hours, days, and years in front of the television in a glazed-over stupor, not thinking or even bothering to have a conversation with a family member.

Starting at the tender ages between two and five, children are already spending an average of twenty-five hours a week watching television. This time is one of the most important stages in a child's life. Children learn more during this period than they do in any other stage of their lives, and television viewing does not assist the learning process. Think about it: A child spends more than an entire day of each week watching television!

As children grow older and start hanging out with their friends, they spend only a little less time watching television. Children between the ages of six and eleven watch more than twenty-two hours of television per week, and teens aged twelve to seventeen watch an average of twenty-three hours of television every week. Teenager's schedules are packed with school, homework, after-school jobs, and extracurricular activities, yet they still find the time to watch television more than twenty hours per week.

According to Newton Minnow, the former chairman of the Federal Communications Commission, "By the time most Americans are eighteen years old, they have spent more time in front of the television set than they have spent in school, and far more than they have spent talking with their teachers, their friends, or even their parents. . . . By first grade, most children have spent the equivalent of three school years in front of the TV set."

In fact, average people who are children today will spend seven years of their lives watching television by the time they reach the age of seventy. That's a lot of wasted time just sitting on a couch staring at a box. Think about how much time you have wasted watching television the next time you reach for the remote control. Remember how much happier you are when you read a book, write in a journal, go out for a bike ride, or even communicate with other real, live people. Try taking a week off from television and you'll be surprised at how much enjoyment you get out of life.

Directions: Think about the topics contained in the passage on the previous page. Finish filling out the graphic organizer below with information from the passage. Think of the graphic organizer as an outline for the information in the passage.

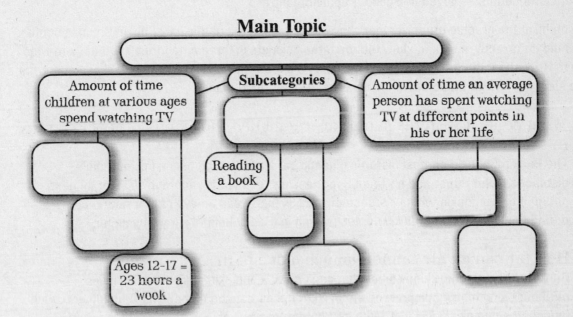

Main Topic

Amount of time children at various ages spend watching TV

Subcategories

Reading a book

Amount of time an average person has spent watching TV at different points in his or her life

Ages 12-17 = 23 hours a week

Subject Review

Not to sound nerdy, but graphic organizers can be a lot of fun. It's like solving a puzzle when you put the right pieces in place. And better yet, it's often much easier to learn something when you see the information displayed in a good graphic organizer.

Did you fill in the graphic organizer that showed the placement of the 2002 Punkin Chunkin contest? If you did it correctly, it should show the top three finishers in three categories in an easy-to-read format. How about the graphic organizer for the *Frying Our Eyes Out* passage? It asked you for the main idea, and then it broke down the major (and supporting) details.

What contest features pumpkins catapulted thousands of feet in the air?

The Punkin Chunkin contest features gigantic catapults hurling pumpkins incredible distances. John Huber and his team Hypertension set a world record in 2002 for longest catapult of a pumpkin with a distance of 1,728.34 feet. Keep an eye out for new records during the next Punkin Chunkin contest, which is usually held in early November.

How far can an air cannon launch a pumpkin?

Air cannons are long, skinny tubes that can power a pumpkin more than 500 miles per hour using highly compressed air. In 2002, the air cannon named 2nd Amendment launched a pumpkin 3,882 feet. With its 120-foot-long barrel, one of its shots in a 2001 competition measured 4,163 feet. The air cannon Big 10 is working on chunking a pumpkin more than a mile—5,280 feet!

About how many hours of television does the average five-year-old watch per week?

A recent study showed that children between the ages of two and five watch about twenty-five hours of television per week. That means over a one-year period, those kids will have watched roughly 1,000 hours of television!

CHAPTER 16
Using Informational Resources

When is the next total solar eclipse going to be visible in the United States?

How did Ludwig van Beethoven change music forever?

When did the first person reach the North Pole?

Can you believe you made it to the last chapter? Congratulations! If you've made it this far, your *Know It All* brain should be almost full to capacity. If you want to fill every nook and cranny of your brain, it will help to know about all of the resources where you can find information. You probably have many of these resources around your home and classroom.

A **dictionary** lists words alphabetically along with their meanings and correct pronunciations. If you wanted to find out the meaning of the word *doppelganger,* for instance, you would use a dictionary. (It means a twin.)

A **thesaurus** lists the synonyms and antonyms of words. If you wanted to find other words to describe being "hungry," for example, you should use a thesaurus. (You'd find "starving," "famished," and "ravenous.") If you wanted to find the opposite of "hungry," you'll see that here too ("full," "sated," and "stuffed").

A **newspaper** is published regularly and contains information about current events. It is usually published daily or weekly.

A **magazine** is a publication that contains stories, articles, pictures, and other entertaining or informative pieces. It is usually published weekly, monthly, or bimonthly.

An **encyclopedia** contains information on a wide range of topics, usually listed alphabetically and sometimes arranged by subject. If you wanted to find more information on spitting frogs, for example, you could look up *frogs* in an encyclopedia.

An **almanac** is a book that contains information regarding the weather, the Moon, the tides, and other related information that was once of interest mainly to farmers who needed to plan their crops. It is published regularly, usually annually.

An **atlas** is a collection of maps. An atlas can contain maps of the world, or road maps of the United States, or any other compilation of maps.

Primary resources are texts and other materials that give firsthand information. For example, photographs, maps, and autobiographies are all primary resources. If your grandfather fought in the Korean War and he told you his firsthand stories from the battlefield, he is a primary resource.

Secondary resources are texts and other materials that give secondhand information that has already interpreted firsthand information. For example, textbooks, encyclopedia articles, and almanacs are all secondary resources.

 **Outer Space Oddities**

Total U.S. Solar Eclipses 2000–2050

A total solar eclipse is a very rare event that occurs when the Moon passes completely in front of the Sun, blocking all sunlight on a part of Earth. The following list shows every total solar eclipse and the location where it will be visible in the United States between 2000 and 2050.

> August 21, 2017: ranging from Oregon to South Carolina
> April 8, 2024: ranging from Texas to Maine
> March 30, 2033: northern Alaska only
> August 23, 2044: only Montana and North Dakota
> August 12, 2045: ranging from California to Florida

▶ Which resource was this information most likely taken from?

A   dictionary
B   magazine
C   atlas
D   almanac

Know It All Approach

This question asks you what informational resource you would find this passage about eclipses. Use what you've learned from the previous page to choose the correct answer choice. If you think you know the right choice, make sure you still read through all the answer choices to make sure.

Go through all the options one by one to see which one fits best. Start with answer choice (A). Is it likely that this passage about eclipses came from the dictionary? A dictionary would define the word *eclipse,* but it wouldn't tell you when the next one is! Cross off answer choice (A) and try the next answer choice.

A magazine may contain an article about eclipses because magazines do contain interesting information. But the article isn't very entertaining; it doesn't contain any pictures, and it isn't much of a "story." Hold onto (B) just in case and try (C) and (D).

Answer choice (C), an atlas, could show you a map of the United States. But it wouldn't tell you when and where a total solar eclipse would be visible. It's not right. So, cross off (C). An almanac, answer choice (D), includes lots of information about stuff like the weather, the Moon, and tides. Wait! If it includes that sort of information, it probably mentions eclipses too! So (D) knocks out (B) for the best answer choice. Answer choice (D) is indeed correct.

Art-rageous

Silent Symphony

Ludwig van Beethoven was born on December 17, 1770, in what is now Germany. He became arguably the greatest musical composer of all time, which is pretty impressive considering that he started to go deaf fairly early on in his career.

Beethoven is regarded as a genius for many reasons, among them being his outstanding ability to communicate vast emotion through his music. His musical included elements of many different styles. He even added voices to one of his symphonies, a feat never before accomplished so successfully.

Some consider Beethoven to have single-handedly lifted music to a higher and more respected level of art. Before his time, music was considered a lesser art form, behind painting and literature. He was a prolific musician, devoting his life to his work. He wrote symphonies, orchestral compositions, chamber music, sonatas, a ballet, an opera, and even a funeral ode for a deceased emperor. In fact, he was one of the first composers to be paid a salary to write whenever and however he wished.

By the time he was thirty-one, Beethoven realized that he was slowly going deaf. For such a gifted musician to lose his hearing was truly a cruel twist of fate. Yet Beethoven refused to let his disability impair his life's role to craft music. He wrote in a letter to a friend in 1802, "I will seize fate by the throat . . . .,"

Ludwig van Beethoven was completely deaf by 1819. His playing nearly ceased, and he became reclusive, rarely leaving his own house. However, he continued to write musical compositions, although he did not write nearly as much as he did during his youth.

After he had lost his hearing, Beethoven spent a great deal of time constructing his final symphony, *The Ninth Symphony,* which many people consider his greatest work of art. The symphony was completed in 1824 and was first performed at the Kärntnertor Theatre, with Beethoven helping to conduct it. Because he was facing the musicians and was turned away from the audience, he did not know what the audience thought of his symphony because he could not hear their reactions. One of his musicians forced him to turn around so that he could see the attendees of the concert applauding passionately.

Directions: Answer questions 1–4 based on the Beethoven passage from page 142.

1. In what source would you most likely find this passage?

    A almanac
    B encyclopedia
    C dictionary
    D thesaurus

2. Is this resource a primary or a secondary source? Explain how you know this.

    _____

    _____

    _____

3. What resource could you use to find another word to use instead of "outstanding" from the second paragraph?

    A thesaurus
    B atlas
    C newspaper
    D dictionary

4. If you don't know the meaning of the word *reclusive* from paragraph three, what resource could help you find the definition? (By the way, *reclusive* means "not inclined to go out or be with other people.")

    A thesaurus
    B atlas
    C newspaper
    D dictionary

April 6, 1909: Peary Discovers the North Pole After Eight Trials in Twenty-Three Years

Commander Robert E. Peary, U.S.N., has discovered the North Pole. Following the report of Dr. F. A. Cook that he had reached the top of the world comes the certain announcement from Mr. Peary, the hero of eight polar expeditions, covering a period of twenty-three years, that at last his ambition has been realized, and from all over the world comes full acknowledgment of Peary's feat and congratulations on his success.

The first announcement of Peary's exploit was received in the following message to *The New York Times:*

Indian Harbor, Labrador, via Cape Ray, N. F., Sept. 6.

The New York Times, *New York: I have the pole, April sixth. Expect arrive Chateau Bay, September seventh. Secure control wire for me there and arrange expedite transmission big story. PEARY*

Following the receipt of Commander Peary's message to *The New York Times* several other messages were received from the explorer to the same effect. Soon afterward, The Associated Press received the following:

INDIAN HARBOR, Via Cape Ray, N. F., Sept. 6—To Associated Press, New York:

Stars and Stripes nailed to the pole. PEARY

To Herbert L. Bridgman, Secretary of the Peary Arctic Club, he telegraphed as follows:

Herbert L. Bridgman, Brooklyn, N.Y.:

Pole reached. Roosevelt safe. PEARY

This message was received at the New York Yacht Club on West forty-fourth street:

INDIAN HARBOR, Via Cape Ray, N.F., Sept. 6 — George A. Carmack, Secretary New York Yacht Club:

Steam yacht Roosevelt, flying club burgee, has enabled me to add North Pole to club's trophies. (signed) PEARY

Directions: Answer questions 5–8 based on the 1909 article about Robert Peary reaching the North Pole.

5. You would probably find this passage in

    A   an almanac

    B   an encyclopedia

    C   a newspaper

    D   an atlas

6. Does this excerpt contain primary resources? Explain how you know this.

    _____

    _____

    _____

7. If you don't know the meaning of the word *expedite* from the article, what resource could help you find the definition? (You'll be happy to know that *expedite* means "to make a task or an event easier.")

    A   thesaurus

    B   atlas

    C   newspaper

    D   dictionary

8. If you wanted to find a word that meant the opposite of the word *hero,* what resource could you use? (One good opposite of *hero* is *villain.*)

    A   thesaurus

    B   atlas

    C   newspaper

    D   dictionary

Subject Review

All right! Sixteen chapters down, zero to go! Your *Know It All* brain is huge! Here are the words from chapter 16 again, just to be sure they are firmly planted in your noggin.

A **dictionary** lists words alphabetically along with their meanings and correct pronunciations.

A **thesaurus** lists the synonyms and antonyms of words.

A **newspaper** is a regularly published paper that contains information about current events. A magazine is a publication that contains stories, articles, pictures, and other entertaining or informative pieces.

An **encyclopedia** contains information on a wide range of topics, usually listed alphabetically and sometimes arranged by subject.

An **almanac** is a book that contains information regarding the weather, the Moon, the tides, and other related information.

An **atlas** is a collection of maps.

Primary resources are texts and other materials that give firsthand information. **Secondary resources** are texts and other materials that give secondhand information and interprets firsthand information.

Now, how about those questions?

When is the next total solar eclipse going to be visible in the United States?

The next total solar eclipse visible in the United States will be in August 21, 2017. It will first be visible in Oregon, but it will also be visible in about ten other states as well.

How did Ludwig van Beethoven change music forever?

Beethoven did things with music that no one had ever done before. He made music into a highly respected art form. He was able to convey emotions and feelings through music in a manner never before accomplished. Beethoven also made the piano a much more appreciated instrument. Music has never been the same since Beethoven began composing.

When did the first person reach the North Pole?

Robert Peary was the first person to reach the North Pole, and he did it on April 6, 1909. You can read the actual *New York Times* article from the next day on page 144!

All About Your Know It All Brain

Your brain is responsible for everything you do. It controls how you walk, how you talk, your heart rate, your breathing, and your dreams. It receives all sorts of information—smells, sounds, sights, and more—and stores it so you can learn and remember. The human brain is able to perform such incredible feats because of its neurons—about 100 billion of them!

Neurons are nerve cells inside your brain. They are the oldest and longest cells in your body. They are similar to the other cells in your body, with one important difference: They can transmit electrochemical signals. This allows them to pass a message to any location in the body.

There are several different types of neurons. Motor neurons carry the signals that tell your body to act. When you move your muscles, for example, motor neurons are telling your muscles to move. Other neurons called sensory neurons take outside information (for example, light and sound) to your brain. Only the brain can understand what the information means. Finally, interneurons connect neurons in the brain to other neurons in your brain and your spinal cord.

There are several main parts in a brain. The brain stem controls the actions that you consider automatic: blood pressure, heart rate, digestion, and so on. The cerebellum is in the back of your brain, and it helps control balance and coordination. The cerebrum is what you normally think of as the brain. It's the large, complex, wrinkly organ that controls emotions and keeps your memories and thoughts. It also brings all the information together from the rest of your organs.

You brain is the most important organ in your body. That's why it's so well protected. The brain is covered with a membrane called mininges. It prevents the brain from rubbing against the skull. Also, the brain actually floats in a sea of liquid! This liquid, called cerebrospinal fluid, cushions the brain.

If you've ever hit your head hard before, your brain may have knocked into the side of your skull. If you did it very hard, you may have caused a concussion. A concussion is when the brain hits the side of your head and gets bruised. Helmets can offer extra protection and help prevent concussions. So take good care of your brain, it's what makes you a know it all.

Directions: Answer questions 1–4 based on your Know It All Brain.

1. Which resource would give you more information about this subject?

   A   a dictionary open to the word *brain*

   B   an encyclopedia of the human body

   C   an atlas of North America

   D   a weekly newspaper

2. Fill in the graphic organizer below to show the different types of neurons.

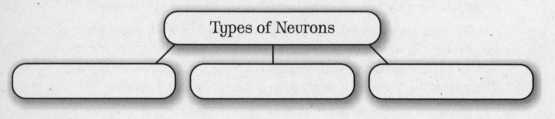

3. What resource could help you find another word that means *important* from paragraph five?

   A   an atlas

   B   an almanac

   C   a thesaurus

   D   a dictionary

4. What can cause a concussion?

   _____

   _____

   _____

   _____

Answers to Chapters and Brain Boosters

Chapter Answer Key

Chapter 1
1. B
2. walls, chandelier, bed
3. C
4. The hotel provides a warm sleeping bag and the hotel puts deer fur on top of the ice.

Chapter 2
1. C
2. A
3. B
4. Many people believe cats were domesticated to protect farms from rodents.
5. The Persian army defeated Memphis by throwing cats over the giant wall that protected the city. Because Egyptians held cats sacred, they surrendered so that the cats wouldn't be hurt.
6. C
7. B
8. C
9. D
10. The fight left Mel Gibson's face bruised and scarred. Because the movie called for a person that looked like this, the fight helped Gibson win the leading role.

Chapter 3
1. D
2. C
3. A
4. B
5. keep
6. Bloodletting meant that a patient's blood was taken out—with the help of bloodsucking leeches.
7. D
8. A
9. B
10. B
11. decent
12. A southpaw is a person who throws a ball left-handed.

Chapter 4

1. A
2. D
3. A
4. There is no way to prove what is "the best" job a person can have. It is only what someone thinks, so it is an opinion.
5. Even though the statement says "in fact," the statement is an opinion. It cannot be proved that something is unattractive because it is just a person's belief.
6. A
7. B
8. The sentence is a fact because it can be proven. You can check the height of the Petronas Towers.
9. D

Brain Booster 1: Review of Chapters 1–4

1. C
2. C
3. D
4. C
5. Many scientists want to send an astronaut to Phobos to study the tiny moon. Also, Phobus could be used as a base to study Mars.

Chapter 5

1. A
2. C
3. Adventurer Steve Fossett wanted to become the first person to float around the world solo in a hot-air balloon. He accomplished this in July 2002, but it was not easy. Each dangerous attempt brought him closer to his goal until he finally succeeded on his sixth attempt.
4. B
5. Eugene has two months to create a science fair project, but he waits until the last minute. When he starts putting a model volcano together, he realizes he doesn't have all the ingredients. He goes to school with a half-completed volcano and searches for the missing pieces. By the time he finishes, the project doesn't work very well, and he gets a D. His teacher tells him to be more prepared.

Chapter 6

1. Zenon became less scared of walking in the woods at night because his older sister explained that the scary things were actually harmless.
2. C
3. The narrator and Zenon will try to catch fireflies in a jar.
4. A
5. The World's Strongest Man competition is a grueling and difficult contest.
6. B
7. C

Chapter 7

1. D
2. B
3. C
4. A
5. C
6. The purpose of this article is to inform people about the *titan arum*. The author uses facts about the flowers to educate readers about the way the flower looks and smells, and how people flock to see it. Its purpose may also be to entertain.
7. A
8. D

Brain Booster 2: Review of Chapters 5–7

1. C
2. B
3. D
4. A concerned girl asks her brother to be safe when he tries to break a silly record.

Chapter 8

1. C
2. A
3. Earth and Venus are roughly the same size.
4. Earth has oxygen in its atmosphere, but Venus does not.
5. D
6. A
7. Both penguins and koalas live in the Southern Hemisphere (in Australia).
8. Koalas live very peaceful lives, sleeping a lot, but penguins live hectic lives, sleeping very little.

Chapter 9

1. D
2. A
3. C
4. The poem is not an example of free verse because the poem uses the structure of stanzas and it also rhymes.
5. A
6. C
7. D
8. B

Chapter 10

1. A
2. C
3. The reader knows it is a flashback because the year goes from 1826 to 1776. Also, John Adams was 90 years old, but in the flashback he is only 40.
4. D
5. A
6. B
7. C
8. "You write it! You are ten times the writer I am."

Brain Booster 3: Review of Chapters 8–10

1. B
2. Huckleberry Finn doesn't like regular schedules or dressing up, but the widow does.
3. This excerpt alludes to *The Adventures of Tom Sawyer*.

Chapter 11

1. The first line of the poem, "I wandered lonely as a cloud" is an example of a simile. It uses the word *as*.
2. B
3. A
4. The phrase in line 12, "Tossing their heads in sprightly dance," is an example of personification because tossing a head is a human action, not something a flower would normally do.
5. C
6. The moth in the poem talks and philosophizes. He craves beauty and gets bored with routine. These are human emotions and demonstrate personification.

Chapter 12

1. C
2. The narrator in the story admired Bobby Fischer very much. You know that he wants to be like Bobby Fischer because he says so.
3. B
4. The story was told by a narrator from outside the story. You know this because it was told from an outside point of view, and the narrator knows how other characters think.
5. Jim Lovell was determined and hard working. You know this because the details in the passage show it. For example, he was ready to focus to save his spacecraft.
6. D

Chapter 13

1. A
2. C
3. The conflict between the monster and the drowning girl's friend changed the monster's character by making him angry toward human beings. The creature tried to save the girl's life, and he was rewarded with a bullet wound. This caused him to vow to hate mankind forever.
4. C
5. D
6. The monster tells Victor Frankenstein about his terrible adventures. The monster saves the life of a girl but is shot as a result.

Brain Booster 4: Review of Chapters 11–13

1. B
2. C
3. D
4. Mohamed Noor Abdullah wanted to break the world record to be famous. (Or he wanted to break his son-in-law's world record.)
5. Abdullah found that the snakes had elected a leader who prevented other snakes from attacking him, but snakes don't really hold elections. This is personification.

Chapter 14

1. C
2. If you cause a spitting cobra to feel threatened, the cobra may spit a stream of venom at your eyes!
3. A hagfish might slime another animal to death if another fish is attacking it.
4. C
5. A
6. B
7. The theremin has influenced recorded music. (The Beach Boys recorded a song using a theremin.) It has also influenced sci-fi movies by providing an eerie soundtrack. It has affected rock and roll, too, because some bands use it in live concerts.

Chapter 15

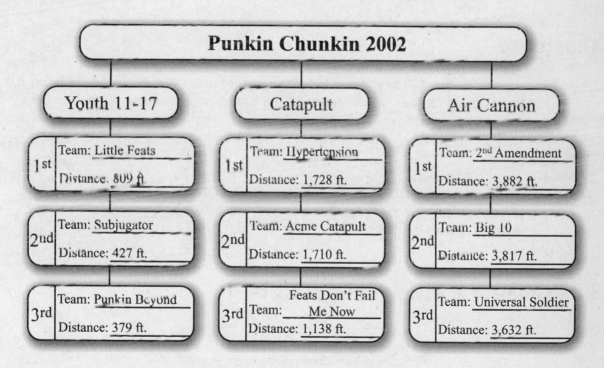

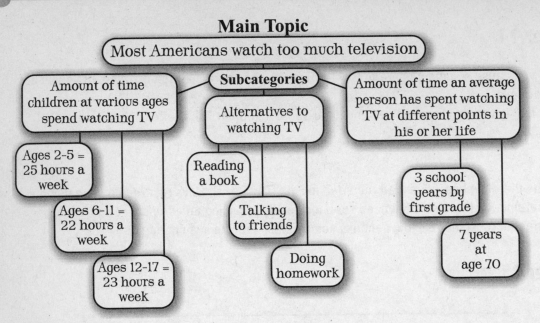

Main Topic

Most Americans watch too much television

Subcategories

Amount of time children at various ages spend watching TV

Alternatives to watching TV

Amount of time an average person has spent watching TV at different points in his or her life

Ages 2-5 = 25 hours a week

Ages 6-11 = 22 hours a week

Ages 12-17 = 23 hours a week

Reading a book

Talking to friends

Doing homework

3 school years by first grade

7 years at age 70

Chapter 16

1. B
2. This resource is a secondary source. You know this because the writer of the passage did not know Ludwig van Beethoven personally. The author used other sources to write the passage, so it must be a secondary source.
3. A
4. D
5. C
6. This resource is a secondary source. You know this because the article is not written from a firsthand point of view. Peary told The New York Times what happened, and the newspaper reported the news.
7. D
8. A

Brain Booster 5: Review of Chapters 14–16

1. B

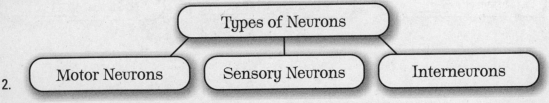

Types of Neurons

Motor Neurons

Sensory Neurons

Interneurons

2.

3. C
4. A hard hit to the head can cause a concussion. The brain hits the side of the skull, and the brain may be bruised.

Know It All!
Practice Test

Introduction to the *Know It All!* Practice Test

By now you've reviewed all the important skills that you should know for middle school reading. You know the difference between fact and opinion (chapter 4). You recognize the handful of important literary and poetic devices (chapters 9 and 10). You learned about the major elements to a story (chapter 13). And these are just a few examples that don't even include all the excellent tidbits of information you've picked up. You *Know It All!*

If you're ready, it's time to try out the skills from the sixteen chapters in this book in a practice test. This test may be similar to a test you take in class. It contains both multiple-choice and open-response questions.

The multiple-choice questions on the test have four answer choices. You should bubble in the correct answer choice on a separate bubble sheet. Cut or tear out the bubble sheet on the next page, and use it for the multiple-choice questions. You can write your answers to the open-response questions directly in the test.

The practice test contains thirty-one questions, twenty-five of which are multiple choice. Give yourself ninety minutes to complete the test.

Take the practice test the same way you would take a real test. Don't watch television, don't talk on the telephone, and don't listen to music while you take the test. Sit at a desk with a few pencils, and have an adult time you if possible. Take the test in one day and all in one sitting. If you break up the test in parts, you won't get the real test-taking experience.

When you've completed the practice test, you may go to page 183 to check your answers. Each question also has an explanation to help you understand how to find the answer. Don't look at that part of the book until you've finished the test!

Good luck!

Answer Sheet

1. Ⓐ Ⓑ Ⓒ Ⓓ
2. Ⓐ Ⓑ Ⓒ Ⓓ
3. Ⓐ Ⓑ Ⓒ Ⓓ
4. Ⓐ Ⓑ Ⓒ Ⓓ
5. use lines provided
6. Ⓐ Ⓑ Ⓒ Ⓓ
7. Ⓐ Ⓑ Ⓒ Ⓓ
8. Ⓐ Ⓑ Ⓒ Ⓓ
9. Ⓐ Ⓑ Ⓒ Ⓓ
10. use lines provided
11. Ⓐ Ⓑ Ⓒ Ⓓ
12. Ⓐ Ⓑ Ⓒ Ⓓ
13. Ⓐ Ⓑ Ⓒ Ⓓ
14. Ⓐ Ⓑ Ⓒ Ⓓ
15. use lines provided

16. Ⓐ Ⓑ Ⓒ Ⓓ
17. Ⓐ Ⓑ Ⓒ Ⓓ
18. Ⓐ Ⓑ Ⓒ Ⓓ
19. Ⓐ Ⓑ Ⓒ Ⓓ
20. use lines provided
21. Ⓐ Ⓑ Ⓒ Ⓓ
22. Ⓐ Ⓑ Ⓒ Ⓓ
23. Ⓐ Ⓑ Ⓒ Ⓓ
24. Ⓐ Ⓑ Ⓒ Ⓓ
25. Ⓐ Ⓑ Ⓒ Ⓓ
26. Ⓐ Ⓑ Ⓒ Ⓓ
27. Ⓐ Ⓑ Ⓒ Ⓓ
28. Ⓐ Ⓑ Ⓒ Ⓓ
29. Ⓐ Ⓑ Ⓒ Ⓓ
30. use lines provided
31. use lines provided

Sample Question

Directions

Read the passage, then read the questions that go with the passage. Find the best answer to the questions and mark the letter for your answer on the bubble sheet. Write the answers to open-response questions directly in the test.

Sample A

Diabolo Practice

Zhou Wen spun his diabolo faster on his string by moving his arms, up and down, faster and higher. The diabolo was invented in China thousands of years ago. It looks like a huge yo-yo, but instead of being attached to a string at one end, the diabolo balances on a string and spins there, while a person holds onto the string at each end. Zhou Wen then flung his diabolo high into the air by throwing both arms up, and it continued to spin in mid air.

Yan Feng, who was standing thirty feet away, caught the diabolo on her string. She whipped the string with her wooden sticks so the ancient toy maintained its spin. Within seconds, Yan Feng had the diabolo balanced on her string, spinning swiftly. "The trick is keeping the diabolo spinning," Yan Feng told her brother. "The faster it spins, the better it stays on the string." She then launched it back toward Zhou Wen.

Zhou Wen missed the diabolo, and it ricocheted off his string, bouncing off the ground "Of course you do have to catch it first," Yan Feng joked.

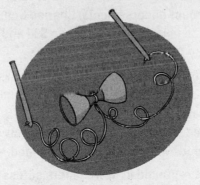

▶ What does the word *swiftly* mean in paragraph two of the passage?

A quickly
B quietly
C slowly
D loudly

You're a Good Man, Charlie Schulz

Snoopy and Charlie Brown are probably the most famous comic-strip personalities ever created. Snoopy, the beagle, and his owner Charlie Brown, the hapless boy, are the main characters in the comic strip *Peanuts,* created by cartoonist Charles Schulz. Schulz used his own life as creative inspiration for Charlie Brown and the *Peanuts* cast. He gave them real feelings, real fears, and real problems—just like in his own life.

Schulz, a native of St. Paul, Minnesota, often felt insecure and lonely when he was young. When he was in junior high school, he was the smallest, youngest student in the class. He felt isolated, like no one really understood or loved him. He used those emotions in his comic strip, and people everywhere identified with it. Unlike other comic strips, which often used silly gags or dramatic action, *Peanuts* presented a personal, philosophical point of view. Charlie Brown was a real character who spoke the truth even when the truth wasn't so funny.

Charles Schulz first published *Peanuts* in 1950, when he was twenty-seven years old. His cartoon grew in popularity over the next fifty years. Eventually, *Peanuts* was printed in 2,600 newspapers in more than twenty languages. Fifty-five million people tuned in to watch the 1969 *Peanuts* television Christmas special. Schulz also sold more than 300 million books. His expressions, "security blanket" and "good grief!", became common terms in American culture.

Peanuts became the most widely read cartoon of all time. And, in part because of many product endorsements, Charles Schulz became the richest cartoonist of all time, making between $30 and $40 million per year. He gave millions away to charities.

Forced to retire in 2000 because of illness, Schulz announced that his last original *Peanuts* strip would be published on Sunday, February 13, 2000. Schulz passed away on the night of February 12, 2000, while the final strip was being printed. Schulz's life had become entwined with the life of *Peanuts*—his life ended when the comic strip ended.

Today, *Peanuts* is reprinted in newspapers across the world. But no new strips are written. Newspapers will only print Schulz's original strips. The adventures of Snoopy, Charlie Brown, Lucy, Pig Pen, Linus, and the gang are charming and entertaining to a whole new generation of fans.

Directions: Answer questions 1–5 based on the passage about Charles Schulz.

1. What does the word *isolated* mean in paragraph two?

   A scared
   B alone
   C artistic
   D original

2. Which of these phrases from the passage contains alliteration?

   A Schulz used his own life as creative inspiration for Charlie Brown.
   B He was the smallest, youngest student in the class.
   C *Peanuts* presented a personal, philosophical point of view.
   D Newspapers will only print Schulz's original strips.

3. What was most likely the author's purpose in writing this passage?

   A to explain why he liked *Peanuts* more than any other comic strip
   B to sell *Peanuts* books and other products
   C to discuss the wealthiest entertainers in the world
   D to offer a history of *Peanuts* and its creator

4. Which of the following best expresses the main idea for this story?

   A Charles Schulz died the night before his last original comic strip was published in a newspaper.
   B Charles Schulz's comic strip was successful because he expressed his own experiences and emotions.
   C *Peanuts* was a very clever and often hilarious comic strip.
   D *Peanuts* earned Charles Schulz millions of dollars, much of which he gave away to charity.

5. Complete the graphic organizer below using information from the passage.

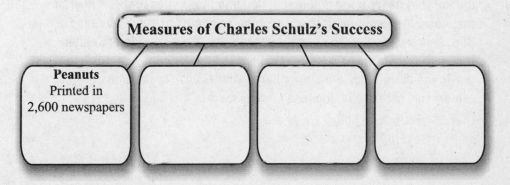

Measures of Charles Schulz's Success

Peanuts
Printed in
2,600 newspapers

The Little Spacecraft That Could

 In 1609, the astronomer Galileo Galilei discovered the four major moons of Jupiter: Callisto, Europa, Io, and Ganymede. So what better name to give an unmanned spacecraft on a mission to explore Jupiter than *Galileo?*

The little twenty-foot *Galileo* began its gargantuan journey of the more than two billion miles to Jupiter in 1989, roaring into space aboard the shuttle *Atlantis.* To cover this vast distance, the *Galileo* would need more than just its own engines to propel it, so it was programmed to use the slingshot effect. This means that it would travel from planet to planet using each planets' gravity to pull it along. So, *Galileo* first went in the opposite direction toward Venus. As it approached Venus, the hot planet's gravity bent *Galileo*'s flight path. The spacecraft was then boosted faster as it flew away from the planet back toward Earth. Then Earth's gravity helped to pull *Galileo* toward Jupiter.

Galileo took many pictures on its way to Jupiter. It took the first up close pictures ever of an asteroid. It took a famous photo of an asteroid called Ida on August 28, 1993. Ida was the first asteroid discovered with its own little travel companion! The floating asteroid had its own little moon, only about a mile long. In making this discovery, *Galileo* had already made history, and it still hadn't reached Jupiter!

Unfortunately, as the journey progressed, not everything worked on the spacecraft as it should. *Galileo*'s main antenna did not open when it was supposed to do. So, the scientists at NASA had to rely on the craft's smaller antenna. That means *Galileo* could not send as much data to Earth as they had hoped. But it could still tell the scientists a wealth of information.

Finally, after traveling for about five years, *Galileo* reached Jupiter, the solar system's largest planet. It became the first spacecraft to orbit the massive gas planet. It took spectacular photos of a comet called Shoemaker–Levy 9 as the comet crashed into the dark side of Jupiter. It also took pictures of the planet's giant red spot, which is actually a hurricane three times the size of Earth. And *Galileo* took some remarkable pictures of Jupiter's famous moons.

Jupiter's four major moons, discovered by Galileo Galilei in 1609, are like separate worlds. Callisto, Europa, Io, and Ganymede are all large and unique moons. *Galileo*'s photos gave clues that three of the moons might have oceans. This has led some scientists to think that life could exist on Jupiter's moons. The pictures also showed Io, the most volcanic body in the known universe. With its giant explosions of lava and gas, Io was an astonishing sight. *Galileo* took pictures of Jupiter's twelve smaller moons, too.

In July 1995, *Galileo* did another incredible feat by releasing a 747-pound probe to land on Jupiter. This mini spacecraft was designed to study Jupiter's atmosphere. The probe began its descent to Jupiter at faster than 100,000 miles per hour! As it entered the planet's atmosphere, it sent information back to *Galileo*. *Galileo* then sent the data to Earth. The data told us about Jupiter's temperature, its clouds, its air pressure, and more. Eventually, the pressure destroyed the tiny probe. The probe taught scientists all kinds of things about Jupiter.

The probe found that Jupiter is very hot. The probe's last recorded temperature was 305 degrees Fahrenheit. And the planet isn't as cloudy as scientists thought it would be. But the winds are even stronger. Below the clouds, *Galileo*'s probe measured the wind at 330 miles per hour. That's faster than most tornados on Earth!

For the next eight years, *Galileo* continued to study Jupiter and its moons. It took thousands of amazing pictures, and it revealed many secrets about the distant worlds. Scientists did not expect the spacecraft to last as long as it did.

In 2003, scientists decided that *Galileo* had accomplished this job, and its mission was over. The spacecraft did not work very well anymore in part because radiation from Jupiter and Io caused some parts to break. The mission experts at NASA agreed to crash the remarkable spacecraft into Jupiter. The scientists could have let it continue to orbit the gigantic planet. But they didn't want it to accidentally crash into one of its moons and disrupt any possible life there.

Galileo crashed into Jupiter in September 2003, ending its wonder-filled fourteen-year journey.

Directions: Answer questions 6–10 about the newspaper article.

6. What is the purpose of the slingshot effect?

   A It shortens the distances from Earth to other planets.
   B It can release probes into other planets.
   C It quickens the speed of spacecraft.
   D It tells about a planet's temperature.

7. Which of the following was *Galileo*'s probe **not** able to find out?

   A Jupiter's weight
   B Jupiter's temperature
   C Jupiter's wind speeds
   D Jupiter's pressure

8. What resource could you use to find a word that means the opposite of *descent* from the passage?

   A a thesaurus
   B an atlas
   C an almanac
   D a dictionary

9. Why did NASA engineers send *Galileo* crashing into Jupiter in 2003?

   A to study the planet's temperature, winds, and clouds
   B because they were tired of working on it for so long
   C because the main antenna wasn't working very well
   D to keep it from crashing on one of Jupiter's moons

10. Do you think that the NASA engineers were pleased with *Galileo*'s performance? Why or why not? Explain your answer on the lines below. Use examples from the passage to support your answer.

_____

_____

_____

_____

_____

_____

_____

_____

_____

_____

_____

_____

_____

_____

_____

_____

It's a Dog's Life

 Dogs are fun and loyal friends. They can play fetch, they can catch Frisbees ™ in their mouths, and they provide entertainment and companionship. People spend many hours and many dollars to give their dogs good lives. But there are special types of dogs that work very hard to improve the lives of humans. Some of these dogs do things that you'll be amazed dogs can do.

Seeing-Eye™ Dogs

Blind people often walk around with a special kind of dog. Seeing-eye™ dogs act like eyes for the blind. With a seeing-eye™ dog, for example, a blind person can cross the street safely. Even though dogs are colorblind and can't understand traffic lights, they will only lead their owners into the street when it is safe for them to cross.

Firedogs

Firedogs are a tradition at firehouses across America. Most people think of a black-and-white spotted Dalmatian as a firedog. Do you know the purpose of these special dogs? Before there were fire trucks, fire carriages had to be pulled by horses. The dogs would help clear the way for the horses by running ahead of them. They helped lead the horses to the fire, and they also calmed the horses down. Now that fire trucks don't use horses anymore, the tradition of firedogs is becoming less common. But many fire fighters still consider their firedogs an important part of the company.

Search-and-Rescue Dogs

If you're skiing or snowboarding and you see an avalanche coming, you'd better hope that there are some dogs nearby. That's because a search-and-rescue dog is one of the best ways to find a person buried by an avalanche. The dogs can smell a victim's scent, even if they are buried by as much as thirty feet of snow! They will dig in the snow when they catch a scent. Search-and-rescue dogs are also trained to find lost people out in the wilderness in the winter or in the summer. For example, a dog can smell the trail of a lost hunter out in the forest up to thirty-six hours after the hunter passes by.

Mine-Detector Dogs

Certain dogs are trained to smell land mines, saving countless lives. They can smell very small quantities of old vapor from the chemicals in the mine. When a mine-detector dog finds a mine, it will sit next to it to alert its owner of the danger. Then people can remove and destroy the mine. In certain situations, dogs can locate deadly mines four times faster than people can. These dogs are real lifesavers!

Sheepdogs

Sheepdogs are one of the most common types of helping dogs. They're used all over the world to help shepherds control their animals. Sheepdogs are alert and smart, and they make sure that sheep don't wander away from the group and get lost. They also watch out for dangerous animals, such as wolves.

Healing Dogs

Dogs have also been known to help people simply feel better. Hospitals are using a new system called "animal therapy" to help sick people recuperate from an illness. Dogs can make people happy, and people often say that laughter is the best medicine. Some dogs have even been able to help disabled children communicate better. These helpful dogs manage to get children to interact in a useful, nonverbal way.

All of these types of dogs have to train and practice regularly to be able to do what they do. Dogs have been helping people for hundreds of years, and they'll continue to help people for many years to come. Their contribution to society cannot be measured, but they certainly deserve our gratitude.

Directions: Answer questions 11–15 based on the passage about the different jobs a dog can have.

11. Why did the author separate the passage into different parts using different headings?

    A to explain how the mine-detecting dog can find land mines
    B to make it easier to read about a few different types of helping dogs
    C to give all the reasons why dogs are the author's favorite animals
    D to list organizations that help different groups of people

12. Which if the following characteristics does **not** describe a sheepdog?

    A rare
    B loyal
    C intelligent
    D protective

13. Read the sentence below from the passage.

    Hospitals are using a new system called "animal therapy" to help sick people recuperate from an illness.

    In the sentence from the passage, what does the word *recuperate* mean?

    A injure
    B fall apart
    C get better
    D be happy

14. What is one way that seeing-eye™ dogs are helpful?

    A They are colorblind and cannot understand traffic lights.
    B They can smell small quantities of dangerous chemicals.
    C They can play catch and are fun to play with.
    D They can help blind people cross streets safely.

15. Complete the following graphic organizer:

dog: _____
job: _____
_____
_____

dog: _____
job: _____
_____
_____

dog: _____
job: _____
_____
_____

Helping Dogs

dog: _____
job: _____
_____
_____

dog: _____
job: _____
_____
_____

dog: _____
job: _____
_____
_____

The following poem is based on a true story of a disappearing ship.

The Phantom Ship

By Henry Wadsworth Longfellow

In Mather's Magnalia Christi,
Of the old colonial time,
May be found in prose the legend
That is here set down in rhyme.

A ship sailed from New Haven,
And the keen and frosty airs,
That filled her sails at parting,
Were heavy with good men's prayers.

"O Lord! if it be thy pleasure"—
Thus prayed the old divine—
"To bury our friends in the ocean,
Take them, for they are thine!"

But Master Lamberton muttered,
And under his breath said he,
"This ship is so crank and walty
I fear our grave she will be!"

And the ships that came from England,
When the winter months were gone,
Brought no tidings of this vessel
Nor of Master Lamberton.

This put the people to praying
That the Lord would let them hear
What in his greater wisdom
He had done with friends so dear.

And at last their prayers were answered:—
It was in the month of June,
An hour before the sunset
Of a windy afternoon,

When, steadily steering landward,
A ship was seen below,
And they knew it was Lamberton, Master,
Who sailed so long ago.

On she came, with a cloud of canvas,
Right against the wind that blew,
Until the eye could distinguish
The faces of the crew.

Then fell her straining topmasts,
Hanging tangled in the shrouds,
And her sails were loosened and lifted,
And blown away like clouds.

And the masts, with all their rigging,
Fell slowly, one by one,
And the hulk dilated and vanished,
As a sea-mist in the sun!

And the people who saw this marvel
Each said unto his friend,
That this was the mould of their vessel,
And thus her tragic end.

And the pastor of the village
Gave thanks to God in prayer,
That, to quiet their troubled spirits,
He had sent this Ship of Air.

16. What is the purpose of the poem?

    A to make the reader laugh

    B to tell a story about a mysterious event

    C to explain how to do something

    D to describe a certain type of ship

17. How does this poem show personification?

    A It gives the clouds life and animation.

    B It uses the same letter at the beginning of many words.

    C It rhymes.

    D It includes dialogue.

18. Which lines of each stanza rhyme with each other?

    A the first and second

    B the first and third

    C the second and third

    D the second and fourth

19. How many stanzas are there in this poem?

    A 2

    B 4

    C 13

    D 14

Top of the World

Allison looked up and could see the peak. She smiled beneath her face mask. Mount Everest, the world's tallest mountain at 29,035 feet, was within her sights. She hiked along the Cornice Traverse, a razor-thin edge of snow and rocks that climbers needed to pass to get to Everest's summit. To her left was a petrifying 8,000-foot drop down the southwest face of Everest. To her right was a terrifying 10,000-foot drop down the Kangshung face of the mountain. There was no room for a mistake. "Only a few hundred vertical feet away now," she hollered to her climbing partner, her sister Laura. Laura trailed behind her by about twenty-five feet.

Too exhausted to respond, Laura took another step toward her sister, stopped, and tried to catch her breath. The two women were at about 28,750 feet, well into what mountain climbers call the "Death Zone." That's the area above around 26,000 feet, where conditions are so poor that most people can't survive for more than a few days. The lack of oxygen at such a high altitude can cause sickness. People can lose focus, get dizzy, or fall victim to a condition called HAPE (high altitude pulmonary edema), which causes the lungs to fill with deadly fluid. The extreme cold and intense winds add another challenge to the high-altitude climb.

Laura caught her breath and took another agonizing step forward. The chilling winds gusted across the narrow ridge at more than seventy-five miles per hour. The temperature was 40 degrees below zero. It was nearly noon, and Laura and Allison had begun their day from Base Camp IV, at 26,000 feet, at midnight. To be successful, they needed to get to the summit and return to Base Camp IV within the day. Too much time above 26,000 feet could prove disastrous.

The bitter cold wind slashed through Laura's thick down jacket, and she couldn't feel her feet. Her mind was foggy and delirious. She sucked on her oxygen tank and pushed forward. Within the hour, she was with her sister at Mount Everest's final obstacle, the Hillary Step.

In 1953, Edmund Hillary and Tenzing Norgay were the first people to climb the steep, exposed, final access to the summit. That's how the treacherous section of the mountain was named. Once past the Hillary Step, climbers can enjoy a relatively gentle hike to the top of the world. Now perched at the base of the Hillary Step, Laura and Allison had to make a decision.

Black clouds were approaching Everest's peak from all directions. Intense winds whipped snow off the summit at a powerful pace. As tiny ice particles stung her eyes, Laura's heart sunk into her stomach. She realized it was unsafe to climb any farther. If a storm hit the mountain when they were on top of it, there would be no way out. It was getting late, and her strength was fading. Laura knew she could make it to the top of the mountain, but she wasn't sure if she could get back. Coming down the mountain can be as difficult as getting up it.

"Ready?" Allison shouted through the wind, starting to climb ahead without waiting for an answer.

"We have to turn back," said Laura, with a look of misery on her face.

"What?" Allison responded. "But we've made in so far! Good grief, Charlie Brown! We can't turn back now—Everest's peak is just ahead!"

Allison and Laura were on their first attempt to scale Mount Everest and reach the top of the world. Their preparation had taken many years, and now they stood only a few hours from achieving their shared goal.

Laura looked up at the approaching clouds. "It's not safe," she said. "If we get caught in a storm above Base Camp IV, we're goners. We need to get back to the base. I know you're disappointed, but—"

"Say no more," her sister interrupted. "You're right. The conditions have to be perfect for this, and they're not. I don't want to put either of us in a risky situation. What good is it to reach the top if we can't make it back to the bottom?"

Laura finally cracked a smile. "Thanks, sis," she said. Laura was frozen to the bone and dizzy, and was turning her back on one of her life's goals. But she knew she was making the right decision. She also knew that she would be back one day to climb to the summit.

Directions: Answer questions 20–25 about the story *Top of the World*.

20. Write a summary of this story.

_____

_____

_____

_____

21. Which of the following will most likely happen next in this story?

   A Allison will climb the Hillary Step while her sister goes back to the base camp.
   B Laura and Allison will attempt to reach the summit before the storm hits Everest.
   C Allison and Laura will head back down the mountain to Base Camp IV.
   D Laura will climb the Hillary Step while her sister goes back to the base camp.

22. Which statement from the passage demonstrates an allusion to another literary work?

   A "Thanks, sis," she said.
   B There was no room for a mistake.
   C Intense winds whipped snow off the summit at a powerful pace.
   D "Good grief, Charlie Brown!"

23. Which of the following statements is an opinion, based on the information in the passage?

   A Mount Everest is the tallest mountain in the world.
   B Mount Everest is the most impressive mountain to climb.
   C Exposure to high altitude can result in illness.
   D The Hillary Step was named after Edmund Hillary.

24. Which point of view is this story told from?

A first person
B second person
C third person
D Laura's point of view

25. To successfully scale Mount Everest, a climber needs to reach the following four stages:

(1) Hillary Step
(2) Base Camp IV
(3) Peak
(4) Cornice Traverse

What is the proper order of the stages, if you were to climb toward the top of the mountain?

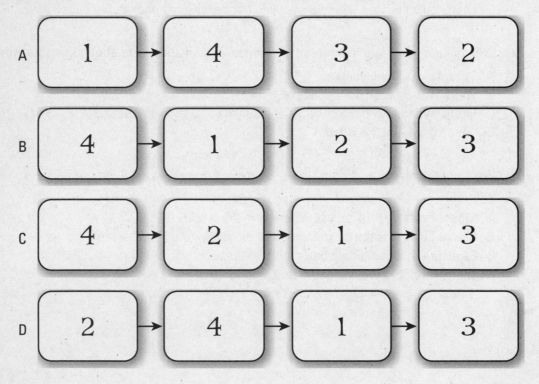

A 1 → 4 → 3 → 2

B 4 → 1 → 2 → 3

C 4 → 2 → 1 → 3

D 2 → 4 → 1 → 3

Frisbee™ Man

How would you like to be turned into a piece of sporting equipment?

Well, Ed Headrick, the inventor of the modern Frisbee™, wanted to be. He was so passionate about his invention that he wanted to *become* a Frisbee after he died. He asked to be cremated and for his ashes to be formed into a series of Frisbees™, which could then be given out to a couple of close friends and family members who can now throw and catch Ed Headrick in parks and at the beach. Hopefully they won't toss him into the sea!

Ed Headrick will be remembered for more reasons than his strange request to be turned into a Frisbee™. He changed the way that a Frisbee™ flies, he was a visionary of the sport, and he even helped to invent a game called disc golf.

In the late 1800s, the Frisbie Baking Company used curved tins for its pies. People found that after they ate the pies, they could throw the tins, and they flew pretty well. That was the first incarnation of the flying disc. In 1948, a man named Walter Frederick Morrison invented the next version of the flying disc. It was plastic, and the outer third edge was sloped. In 1951, he called a version of it the Pluto Platter. (UFOs were very popular at the time.) However, it wasn't until Ed Headrick entered the picture that the flying disc's popularity took off!

Ed Headrick, an inventor for the toy company Wham-O™, changed the design for the flying disc in the early 1960s. He added aerodynamic elements to the design to make it fly farther and better. He added grooved lines to the top of the disc, which made the disc fly straighter and with less wobble. That featured earned Ed Headrick the nickname "Steady Eddie." The name "Frisbee" was also trademarked based on name of the old, now-closed, baking company.

With the new parts added to the flying disc, the design was complete. Wham-O™ advertised the Frisbee™ as a new sport, and the new invention became very popular. Ed Headrick was philosophical about the Frisbee™. He said it had a spirit. He said Frisbee™ was a religion.

So in 1969, Headrick founded the International Frisbee™ Association. By 1975 more than 110,000 members joined to share in their love for the Frisbee™. In 1976 he founded the Professional Disc Golf Association, and helped come up with the game of disc golf.

The idea of disc golf is similar to regular golf. Disc golfers throw a Frisbee™ and try to hit a target very far away. However, the target in disc golf is a metal cage, not a hole in the ground like it is for regular golf. It can take a few throws to reach the target in disc golf, and there are many targets on a course. Ed Headrick designed the first disc golf course in Pasadena, California. He designed more than 200 disc golf courses in total.

Today about two million people play disc golf on nearly 1,000 courses in the United States. Disc golf is one of the fastest-growing sports in the country, and Ed Headrick is responsible for it. Today Headrick's Frisbee™ has sold more than 200 million units. He also invented the Super Ball™, which sold more than twenty million units. (His ashes were not made into any super bouncy Super Balls™, however!)

Even though Eddie Headrick died in August 2002, his legacy continues to fly— literally and figuratively.

Directions: Answer questions 26–31 based on the passage about the inventor of the Frisbee™.

26. Ed Headrick earned the nickname "Steady Eddie" by

  A inventing many interesting toys for Wham-O.
  B forming the International Frisbee™ Association.
  C altering the Frisbee's™ design to make it fly better.
  D being turned into several stable, solid Frisbees™.

27. Which statement would Ed Headrick most likely have agreed with?

  A The flight of a Frisbee™ is a beautiful thing.
  B Golf is a lot more fun than disc golf.
  C The original Frisbie Pie version of the flying disc was best.
  D Everybody should be turned into sporting equipment.

28. What resource could you use to find the location of Pasadena, California?

  A an almanac
  B an atlas
  C a dictionary
  D a thesaurus

29. What statement about the Ed Headrick is an opinion?

  A He invented the modern Frisbee™.
  B His ashes were made into Frisbees™.
  C He was the best Frisbee™ player.
  D He designed the first disc golf course.

30. Below, write one difference and one similarity between regular golf and disc golf.

_____

_____

_____

_____

_____

31. What are four of Eddie Headrick's accomplishments? Use complete sentences in your answer.

_____

_____

_____

_____

_____

_____

_____

_____

Answers and Explanations for the Know It All! Practice Test

Answers and Explanations for the *Know It All* Practice Test

1. **B** This question asks you to figure out what the word *isolated* means from paragraph two. Go back to the paragraph in question and read it over. Then read the answer choices to see which one fits best.

   (A) The paragraph says that Charles Shulz was the smallest person in his class, and he felt that no one really understood or loved him. Does that mean he felt *scared*? It could. Hold onto this choice and try the others.
   (B) If *isolated* means *alone,* then the sentence would read, "He felt alone, like no one really understood or loved him." If no one loved you, would you feel alone? Sure, anyone might. (B) is a better answer choice than (A). Check the others.
   (C) and (D) Would these two sentences make any sense in the paragraph?
   "He felt artistic, like no one really understood or loved him.
   "He felt original, like no one really understood or loved him.
   No, right? Cross them off.

2. **C** Alliteration is the repeated sounds at the beginning of words. Just look for the same letter that begins several words in a sentence. Answer choices (A), (B), and (D) don't really show that. Answer choice (C), however, has eight words—five of which start with the letter P!

3. **D** This question asks you to find the author's purpose in writing the passage. Why do you think he or she wrote it? Compare your idea with the answer choices. The purpose must relate to the whole passage, not just one part.

   (A) Did the passage explain why *Peanuts* is better than other comic strips? Well, it explained what made *Peanuts* so good, but it didn't focus on other comics. That wasn't the author's purpose.
   (B) Does the author write the passage to sell *Peanuts* books and products? The passage doesn't tell you where to buy anything or give you prices. It therefore probably isn't trying to sell you something.
   (C) The passage says that Charles Schulz was among the richest entertainers in the world. But is the *purpose* of the passage to discuss rich entertainers?
   (D) Did the passage give a history of *Peanuts*? Did it give reasons for its popularity? Yes and yes. (D) is a good answer choice, and it's correct.

4. **B** Back in chapter 5, you learned that a main idea is what the passage is *mostly* about. Remember that it is not about only one detail.

(A) That Charles Schulz died before his last strip was published is a detail from the passage. It's not what the whole passage was about, so it's not the main idea.

(B) The passage often mentions how Schulz used his own emotions in *Peanuts.* That made it successful. That seems to be what the passage is about. As always, check all the choices to be sure.

(C) The passage doesn't discuss if or how *Peanuts* was hilarious. It can't be the main idea then.

(D) Charles Schulz gave away millions of dollars to charity. That's true, but this is only a detail from the passage. If the passage were about his donations, this could be the main idea. But it's not.

5. Here is your first open-response question! And it's a graphic organizer question, to boot. You are asked to complete the organizer with information that shows how successful Charles Schulz was. One box is already filled in with "printed in 2,600 newspapers." You have to fill in the other three boxes. How else was Charles Schulz successful? Use information from the passage.

There are many answers that you could write in the boxes to get credit. For example, you could write that *Peanuts* ran for fifty years. Or that Charles Schulz became the richest cartoonist of all time. You could also write that *Peanuts* became the most widely read cartoon of all time. Other answers could be "fifty-five million people tuned in to watch his Christmas special, "sold more than 300 million books," or "his expressions became common terms of American culture."

6. **C** The second paragraph of this passage tells about the slingshot effect. It says that as the spacecraft approaches a planet, the planet's gravity bends its flight path. Then the spacecraft is boosted faster away from the planet. That fits with answer choice (C). Be careful with answer choice (A); the effect may cause the spacecraft to get to other planets faster, but it actually adds more distance! Answer choices (B) and (D) relate to *Galileo*'s probe, which did not use the slingshot effect.

7. **A** You have to find the information that *Galileo*'s probe did **not** find. Watch out for that "**not**"! Read the section about *Galileo*'s probe again. You can cross off any choices that tell information that the probe found out.

(A) The probe didn't find out about Jupiter's weight. Hold onto this choice.
(B) *Galileo*'s probe measured Jupiter's temperature at 305 degrees Fahrenheit. Because it did find this information, you can cross it off. (Remember, you're looking for something the probe did **not** find!)
(C) You learned in the passage that the winds of Jupiter are faster than tornados on Earth! The probe measured that. Therefore, you can cross off answer choice (C).
(D) A sentence from the passage says, "The data told us about Jupiter's temperature, its clouds, its air pressure, and more." Cross off (D). You're left with answer choice (A)!

8. **A** Maybe you had trouble with the word *descent*. It's a tough word. If you wanted to know what it means, you could look it up in a dictionary. But this question asks you what resource to use to find the *opposite* of the word! A thesaurus, answer choice (A), will tell you words that mean the same or words that mean the opposite. That's why (A) is the correct answer choice.

9. **D** The end of *Galileo*'s mission is explained in the last paragraph. Read it again before checking out the answer choices.

(A) *Galileo*'s probe studied Jupiter's temperature, winds, and clouds. But that doesn't explain why NASA engineers wanted to destroy it! Answer choice (A) isn't right.
(B) There is no information in the passage that says that NASA engineers were tired. Besides, what kind of excuse is that?
(C) Yes, the antenna on *Galileo* did not work very well. But that happened early in the spacecraft's mission. Even though the main antenna was broken, the smaller antenna was used to send pictures of asteroids, Jupiter, and Jupiter's moons. The broken antenna was not the reason why the spacecraft was sent crashing into Jupiter.
(D) Some NASA engineers think there could be life on Jupiter's moons. And if there is life, the people at NASA don't want to disrupt it. Yes, this is the right choice!

10. This question requires you to write a long response to an open-response question. Remember to use information from the passage. Notice that the question asks you to explain your answer. Therefore, you should use as much information as you can. Below is a sample response that would likely earn you full credit.

> The NASA engineers were probably very pleased with Galileo's performance. While there were some problems with it, Galileo also did some amazing things. Galileo took some great pictures of asteroids. It even took a picture of an asteroid with its own moon! Then when it got to Jupiter, it took lots of pictures. It took pictures of Jupiter's big spot and its moons too. Galileo also dropped a probe into Jupiter's atmosphere. That told scientists a lot of information, such as the planet's temperature and the speed of its winds. Overall, the spacecraft Galileo taught people a lot about space. And the spacecraft lasted longer than the scientists thought it would. So the NASA engineers were probably very happy with their spacecraft.

11. **B** Notice that the passage about helping dogs is broken down into different parts. Look at each part and try to figure out how that organization helps the passage.

(A) One section of the passage tells how mine-detecting dogs can find land mines. But that's not why the author separated the passage into different parts!
(B) Do the different parts of the passage help to summarize different types of helping dogs? Yes, so that could be why the author created the passage that way. Hold onto this choice and check the rest.
(C) The author doesn't say that dogs are his or her favorite animals! The author only says that dogs are fun, loyal, and helpful. Even if dogs are *your* favorite animal, you shouldn't pick this choice. If it isn't in the passage, it can't be the answer.
(D) Healing dogs help socially disabled children to communicate better. But that explains one type of helping dogs—not why the passage was broken up into sections! The author didn't separate the passage to help disabled children, so you can cross off answer choice (D).

12. **A** This question asks you to find a word that does **not** describe a sheepdog. Go back to the section in the passage called "Sheepdogs." If a description matches an answer choice, cross it off.

(A) The first sentence in the sheepdog section says, "Sheepdogs are one of the most common types of helping dogs." That's not rare at all! Because rare does **not** describe a sheepdog, hold onto this answer choice.
(B) Sheepdogs will stay with lost sheep for days, so they are very loyal! That means you can cross off answer choice (B).
(C) The passage says that sheepdogs are smart, so (C) isn't right either.
(D) Sheepdogs make sure that sheep don't get lost or killed by other animals, so they're very protective! Because "protective" **does** describe sheepdogs, cross it off.

13. **C** Recuperate is a tough word. Fortunately, you can use clues to figure out what it means! Animal therapy is a good thing. So, therapy helps people *do what* from an illness? Try the answer choices.

(A) Could animal therapy help sick people *injure* from an illness? That doesn't make sense! Cross off (A).
(B) Could animal therapy help sick people *fall apart* from an illness? Huh? No.
(C) Could animal therapy help sick people *get better* from an illness? Yes, that makes a lot of sense! If you didn't know *recuperate* means, you can still tell that this seems to fit.
(D) Would you *be happy* from an illness? Probably not, so this answer choice doesn't make sense either!

14. **D** You have to pick the choice that says why seeing-eye™ dogs are helpful. Read the section about them in the passage again. Then go through the choices.

(A) It's true that dogs are colorblind and cannot understand traffic lights. But does that make them *helpful?* No way.
(B) This question asks about seeing-eye™ dogs, not mine-detecting dogs. Cross off answer choice (B).
(C) Dogs can play catch and can be fun, but the passage doesn't say that about seeing-eye™ dogs.
(D) The passage *does* say that seeing-eye™ dogs can help blind people cross the street safely. Therefore, answer choice (D) is correct.

15. Here's another graphic organizer question. This one asks you to fill in six types of helping dogs. You have to write the types of dog *and* what they do. Here is an example of how it could look for full credit.

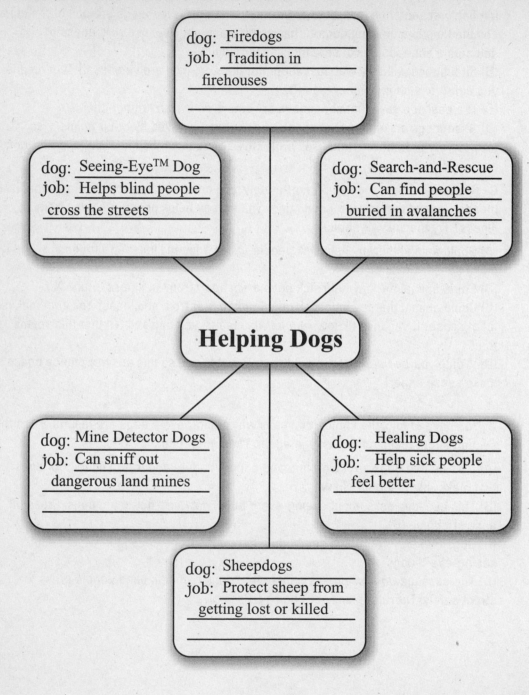

dog: Firedogs
job: Tradition in
    firehouses

dog: Seeing-Eye™ Dog
job: Helps blind people
    cross the streets

dog: Search-and-Rescue
job: Can find people
    buried in avalanches

Helping Dogs

dog: Mine Detector Dogs
job: Can sniff out
    dangerous land mines

dog: Healing Dogs
job: Help sick people
    feel better

dog: Sheepdogs
job: Protect sheep from
    getting lost or killed

16. **B** To find the purpose of the poem, think about what you learned from it. Check the answer choices to see which one makes the most sense.

(A) Did this poem make you laugh? Unless you have a very strange sense of humor, it probably didn't. (It's not supposed to be funny.) Therefore, cross off answer choice (A).
(B) Did the poem tell a story about a mysterious event? Even if you didn't understand the poem, maybe you could tell it was a story. In fact, it was based on a true story about a ship that sunk—only to reappear a year later as a cloud!
(C) What did you learn how to do? Did you learn to cook guacamole or make a paper airplane? The poem didn't really explain how to do something, so (C) is wrong.
(D) The poem describes a ship, so this sounds possible. But is the *purpose* of the poem to describe a certain type of ship? Not exactly. Otherwise there would have been more details about the ship.

17. **A** Personification is the act of giving human qualities to nonhuman things. (Go back to Chapter 11 if you want to review it.) Of all the answer choices, only answer choice (A) is an example of personification. By giving the clouds the appearance of people and faces, William Wadsworth Longfellow uses personification. Answer choice (B) seems to define alliteration.

18. **D** Read each verse to yourself and figure out which lines rhyme. The last line rhymes with the second line. That makes answer choice (D) correct; the second and the fourth lines rhyme.

19. **C** A stanza is a grouping of lines in a poem. Not all stanzas are the same length, but in this case they are. Each stanza is four lines. Count the number of stanzas in this poem over the two pages, and you should end up with thirteen. That's the answer, making answer choice (C) correct.

20. This story is about two sisters who attempt to climb Mount Everest, the world's tallest mountain. A summary includes all the major points to a story, but it doesn't need all of the details. Here is a sample summary that would earn full credit.

> Two sisters, Allison and Laura, are climbing up near the top of Mount Everest. The oxygen is thin and the conditions are dangerous. As Allison and Laura got to the Hillary Step, they have to decide whether to go on. Allison wants to go up, but Laura thinks it's too dangerous. (Dark clouds were approaching, and it was getting late.) Allison realizes her sister is right. It's not worth risking their lives to get to the top.

21. **C** Use what you know from the passage to make a prediction. Laura is tired and weary. She convinces her sister that it's too dangerous to try to make it to the top of the mountain. Which answer choice makes the most logical sense? It's answer choice (C); both sisters will most likely head back down the mountain to Base Camp IV.

22. **D** Remember what you learned in the first passage of this practice test. Also remember that an allusion is a reference to another piece of literature or another passage. "Good grief!" is a common expression used by Charlie Brown, the comic strip character invented by Charles Schulz. The use of that expression in this story is an allusion to *Peanuts.*

23. **B** This is a question that tests you on the difference between fact and opinion. Remember that facts can be proven. Opinions cannot be proven.

(A) It is true that Mount Everest is the tallest mountain in the world. It is 29,035 feet tall. No mountain is taller. Because this can be proven, it is a fact. Cross it off.
(B) Mount Everest is impressive, but the passage does not say it is the *most* impressive to climb. You can't prove that one mountain is the *most* impressive. It is an opinion.
(C) and (D) These answer choices list facts. You know this because they can be proven. High altitude causes many people to get sick. And it is a fact that the Hillary Step was named after Edmund Hillary, the first person to summit Mount Everest.

24. **C** You have to figure out the point of view of the story to answer this question. Is it told from a character in the story, using words like *I* or *me*? No, it is told from an outside perspective. That means it's told from the third-person point of view, answer choice (C).

25. This sequence question forces you to put the stages of Everest in height order. This can be tricky because Allison and Laura are already past Base Camp IV when they start. Use what you know, and get rid of answer choices that must be wrong.

    The story begins with the two sisters climbing up on the Cornice Traverse. They then get to the Hillary Step. Therefore, you know that (4) must come before (1). That means you can get rid of answer choice (A). Answer choice (A) also lists the peak *lower* than the base camp! The Hillary Step is the last major obstacle to get to the peak, so (1) should come right before (3). That means you can get rid of answer choice (B). If you remembered that the sisters began their day of climbing at Base Camp IV, then you know (2) should be the first stage in this sequence. Answer choice (D) shows the proper sequence in order to reach the top of Mount Everest.

26. **C** Go back to the passage and look for the term "Steady Eddie." Then read why he was given that nickname, and compare the answer choices.

    (A) Ed Headrick did invent a lot of useful things. But is that why he got his nickname? The passage doesn't say that, so answer choice (A) isn't correct.
    (B) Yes, Ed Headrick formed the International Frisbee™ Association. But how does that relate to being "steady"? It doesn't. Cross off answer choice (B).
    (C) The fourth paragraph in the passage says that Ed Headrick added grooved lines to the top of the disc. This made the disc fly with less wobble. That's how he got his nickname!
    (D) Ed Headrick got his nickname before he was turned into Frisbees™. Although this choice may seem to fit, the passage says that answer choice (C) is the real reason.

27. **A** Remember that Ed Headrick was a big Frisbee™ freak. He was passionate about Frisbees™, and he even said that Frisbee™ was a religion. Based on that knowledge, pick the choice that fits best with that philosophy.

(A) Yes, Steady Eddie would likely have agreed that the flight of a Frisbee™ was beautiful. Hold this answer choice and try the rest.
(B) Would the creator of disc golf agree that regular golf is more fun? Probably not, so answer choice (B) is incorrect.
(C) Ed Headrick changed the design of the Frisbee™ so it would fly better. He most certainly wouldn't agree that the original "Frisbie Pie" design was best!
(D) While Headrick was turned into a series of Frisbees™, there's no reason to believe he thought that *everybody* should be turned into sporting equipment too. Answer choice (A) is better.

28. **B** An atlas will show you where places are located. That means you could use an atlas to find Pasadena, California. None of the other resources listed would help you find its location. An almanac tells you about tides and the weather. A dictionary defines words and tells you their meanings. A thesaurus gives you other words that mean the same (or the opposite) of a word.

29. **C** Remember that a fact can be proven. An opinion can't be proven. Opinions often use words like *most, best, worst,* or *should.*

(A) Ed Headrick invented the modern Frisbee™. That's a fact. Cross it off.
(B) Ed Headrick's ashes were turned into Frisbees™. It may be hard to believe, but it can be proven. Choice (B) is not an opinion, so it's wrong.
(C) Ed Headrick was probably very good at Frisbee™. But was he the *best*? How can you *prove* that someone is the best? You can't, really, so this is an example of an opinion.
(D) It is a fact that Ed Headrick designed the first disc golf course. It is in Pasadena, California, and he designed it in the mid 1970s.

30. This compare-and-contrast question asks you to write what's different—and what's similar—between golf and disc golf. Use information from the passage for your answer. And don't forget to list both a difference *and* a similarity. Here is an example of a response that would be worth full credit.

Golf and disc golf are similar because in both games you have to reach a target

very far away. Golf and disc golf are different because the target in golf is a hole

in the ground, but the target in disc golf is a metal cage.

31. This final question on the practice test is open response. You have to write four of Eddie Headrick's accomplishments. Reread the passage if it helps you to remember what he did. Be sure to list four things; you will lose points if you only write two or three. Below are eight sample responses. You only needed to write four, but any four of the following answers would be correct.

Ed Headrick invented the modern Frisbee™.
Ed Headrick founded the International Frisbee™ Association.
Ed Headrick is one of the founders of disc golf.
Ed Headrick founded the Professional Disc Golf Association.
Ed Headrick designed the first disc golf course.
Ed Headrick designed more than 200 disc golf courses.
Ed Headrick's Frisbee™ has sold more than 200 million units
Ed Headrick invented the Super Ball™, which has sold more than twenty million units.

The Princeton Review

Partnering With You to Measurably Improve Student Achievement

Our proven 3-step approach lets you **assess** student performance, **analyze** the results, and **act** to improve every student's mastery of skills covered by your State Standards.

Assess
Deliver formative and benchmark tests

Analyze
Review in-depth performance reports and implement ongoing professional development

Act
Utilize after school programs, course materials, and enrichment resources

If students need to know it, it's in our Know It All! Guides!

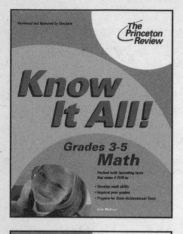

Know It All!
Grades 3–5 Math
0-375-76375-9 • $14.95

Know It All!
Grades 3–5 Reading
0-375-76378-3 • $14.95

Know It All!
Grades 6–8 Math
0-375-76376-7 • $14.95

Know It All!
Grades 6–8 Reading
0-375-76379-1 • $14.95

Know It All!
Grades 9–12 Math
0-375-76377-5 • $14.95

Know It All!
Grades 9–12 Reading
0-375-76374-0 • $14.95